Automatic Pistol Shooting Together with Information on Handling the Duelling Pistol and Revolver

Walter Winans

Alpha Editions

This edition published in 2022

ISBN: 9789356158702

Design and Setting By

Alpha Editions
www.alphaedis.com

Email - info@alphaedis.com

As per information held with us this book is in Public Domain.

This book is a reproduction of an important historical work. Alpha Editions uses the best technology to reproduce historical work in the same manner it was first published to preserve its original nature. Any marks or number seen are left intentionally to preserve.

Table of Contents

PREFACE	- 1 -
CHAPTER I	- 3 -
CHAPTER II	- 5 -
CHAPTER III	- 7 -
CHAPTER IV	- 9 -
CHAPTER V	- 13 -
CHAPTER VI	- 22 -
CHAPTER VII	- 24 -
CHAPTER VIII	- 27 -
CHAPTER IX	- 29 -
CHAPTER X	- 34 -
CHAPTER XI	- 41 -
CHAPTER XII	- 42 -
CHAPTER XIII	- 44 -
CHAPTER XIV	- 46 -
CHAPTER XV	- 53 -
CHAPTER XVI	- 55 -
CHAPTER XVII	- 57 -

CHAPTER XVIII	- 62 -
CHAPTER XIX	- 64 -
CHAPTER XX	- 70 -
FOOTNOTE	- 72 -

PREFACE

Though my last edition of *Hints on Revolver Shooting* was published only four years ago, I find it now necessary, owing to the advance of the automatic pistol, to revise it thoroughly and to add new chapters.

Till quite recently, the automatic pistol had many defects, both as to balance and as to safety, chiefly in the latter respect, so that only a very careful expert could handle one without danger to the public and to himself.

This has now been altered, and with safety bolts and external hammers several automatic pistols are quite safe for the use of experts.

They are still very dangerous in the hands of ignorant persons; a revolver is dangerous enough in such cases but the automatic is much more so.

I shall try to explain how any one possessing mechanical knowledge can, by observing certain precautions, safely carry and shoot an automatic pistol. Of course, some men who, for years, have shot small game, and who are good shots, are still very careless in handling a gun. Such men should never touch an automatic pistol.

I have made the above remarks as I do not want to be responsible for any accidents with automatics; and I advise any one not sure of himself to confine himself to revolvers and single-shot pistols.

The automatic pistol is gradually replacing the revolver except as a gallery pistol.

Up to the present no automatic pistol can shoot gallery, or light-charge, ammunition, and the full charge, because of the noise, is very unpleasant in a shooting-gallery.

It is a great pity that the .44 Smith & Wesson break-down model of revolver (shooting gallery ammunition) is no longer made, as it is still the best revolver for gallery shooting.

M. Gastinne Renette, of 39 Avenue d'Antin, Paris, for his gallery, uses them still, together with his duelling pistols of the same calibre and powder charge.

I mention this as he is the only dealer who can now supply the old Smith & Wesson revolvers.

WALTER WINANS.

17 Rue de Tervueren,
BRUSSELS, BELGIUM.

CHAPTER I

THE AUTOMATIC PISTOL

THIS is the pistol of the future and the revolver has now to give place to it, just as the horse has to give place to the automobile for traction purposes.

Still, like the horse, the revolver seems still to have before it a future for certain purposes, and one uses a revolver where one would not care to use an automatic pistol.

The superiority of the revolver consists in its being adaptable to reduced charges and also in its being less complicated and less apt to be discharged accidentally by an ignorant person.

At one time, the revolver was considered the most dangerous fire-arm in existence, but the automatic far surpasses it in this respect. When the chambers of a revolver are emptied, it is harmless; but when the magazine is taken out, after an automatic pistol has been charged, *one cartridge still remains in the chamber.* This has been the cause of several accidents; a man thinks the pistol is safe after he has extracted the magazine.

The automatic pistol is barred from gallery shooting by the fact that the mechanism is operated by the recoil from a full-charge cartridge only, and this full charge makes too much noise.

I do not advise the purchase of any automatic pistol which does not have at least one safety bolt and which does not have also an external hammer.

There are two makes which, from personal experience, I can recommend; one is the Colt .45 which has been adopted by the United States Government for army and navy purposes. This has a grip at the proper angle for shooting. Hardly any other automatic pistol is properly designed in this respect, their grips being too much at a right angle, so that the barrel tends to point too high, this creating a strain on the wrist, since the wrist must be held in an unnatural position.

The Colt automatic of the U. S. Army pattern has a stock as pleasant to aim with as a duelling pistol.

Next, it has a hammer which can be put to full and half cock, just like that of an ordinary pistol or revolver.

It has, besides, two safety appliances; one a slide which can be moved with the thumb just before firing, like the safety bolt of a shotgun, the other a safety bolt which is pressed by the palm of the hand in the act of squeezing the trigger, like that of the Smith & Wesson safety revolver, later described.

The pistol is, therefore, as "fool-proof" as it seems possible to make it, but yet there is the danger of a cartridge being left in the chamber when the magazine is taken out. I again warn all shooters of automatic pistols to bear this fact constantly in mind whenever handling an automatic.

However, I do not like the sights of this Colt automatic. The front sight is a black, upright, narrow rod when aiming, and the notch in the hind sight is far too small. This arrangement of sights may be all very well for deliberate aiming at a black bull's-eye on a white target, but it is of no use for practical shooting in a bad light.

The front sight should be a "shotgun" silver "bead," and the hind sight a large "U"-shaped notch that will show the full bead in it with a little to spare at the sides.

With these alterations, I think the U. S. Regulation Colt automatic is the best automatic I know.

The Savage automatic is also very good, and I can confidently recommend it, especially for those who find the .45 Colt too large for their purpose.

The following chapters on learning to shoot with the revolver and duelling pistol apply equally to the automatic pistol, except that the butts to be shot against should be more solid when using the automatic, owing to its penetration, and the shooting with it should take place only out-of-doors, as the noise is very bad for indoors.

CHAPTER II

SELECTING A PISTOL

YOU must first decide for what purpose you want the pistol; a "general utility" one is about as much use as a hunter who goes in harness—not much good for either purpose. If you want a hunter, buy an English hunter; if a harness horse, buy an American trotter. In the same way, for whatever purpose you want a pistol, buy one, if by any means you can do so, especially for that purpose. Anyhow, it is useless to compete with a short-barrelled pocket automatic against target pistols. This class of pistol is intended only for self-defence at short range, and has no pretensions to accuracy.

A long barrel theoretically gives greater accuracy, especially at long range, owing to there being more length to burn the powder in, and to the sights being farther apart, which minimizes error in aiming; but practically this advantage is more than counterbalanced by making the pistol heavy at the muzzle, so that it therefore balances badly. The balance ought to be as near the trigger as possible. For a pocket pistol, a short barrel may be absolutely necessary for portability. In England some men use very long barrels, but I prefer shorter pistols, and I do not consider that anything over $7\frac{1}{2}$ inches is a "Military" revolver nor should it be permitted in military competitions.

See that the trigger-pull is "sweet," and has no "drag." Also, have your trigger-pull as light as can safely be used. The pull is often left by makers very heavy, so as to be alterable to suit customers, and the shopman may forget to have this altered. If you are not hampered by rules, about three or three and a half pounds is the best trigger-pull for general purposes.

I do not like a double-action revolver, except for a pocket one, as it cannot do accurate shooting when cocking with the trigger.

For a man whose hands are apt to get moist, roughing the trigger may prevent slipping; but it may also make the finger sore if roughed too sharp.

Some pistols have too narrow a trigger, almost like a piece of wire; a wide, spoon-shaped trigger is best, as less likely to cut the finger, especially when coupled with a heavy trigger-pull.

Get a pistol which, when you grip the stock properly, has the barrel and your arm as nearly in a horizontal line as possible. Many makes of revolvers and automatic pistols have the stock much below the level of the barrel, which consequently is above the hand. This makes shooting more difficult; you are apt to cant the weapon to one side, and the recoil is more severe on your wrist. A man who holds a pistol properly does not need a big stock, even if he has a big hand.

For rough work, and in strong sunlight, a pistol is best blued. I temporarily paint the rib, etc., when target shooting on sunny days, with "sight-black."

Revolver ammunition is usually made in the following calibres: .32, .38, .41, .44, .45, .455. Most of these can be had loaded with various smokeless powders, as King's semi-smokeless, Riflite, Cordite, Walsrode, etc.

The Union Metallic Cartridge Company, U. S. A., have supplied me with great quantities of .44 "gallery ammunition," loaded with both round and semi-round bullets. These have a small charge of black powder, and I should prefer this ammunition out of a Smith & Wesson Russian Model revolver for self-defence, as well as for competitions up to twenty yards, and I find it the most accurate for exhibition shooting. I believe most professional stage-shooters use it. It is a great pity this revolver is no longer made and can only be bought second-hand. If a second-hand one is otherwise good, a new barrel can be put to it. I suppose the various English makers of ammunition could supply "gallery" charges in any of their various calibre cartridges, but I know of none and should not advise the beginner to try loading this sort of ammunition in English cartridge-cases for himself. The dome of the cap is generally higher than in American cartridges; if, therefore, the small powder charge used in gallery ammunition be put in the case and the bullet pressed down, the bullet will come down on the dome, stop up the flash-hole, and cause a misfire. The way to obviate this is to take a wad of suitable calibre, make a hole in the centre, and push the wad down to the bottom of the cartridge before putting in the powder, so as to fill up the base of the cartridge and let the bullet "seat" on the powder, higher than the dome. Makers can do this properly, but an amateur may put the wad in too loosely, and a little powder get under the wad. The result would be that, on the shot being fired, the wad would be driven half-way up the barrel, and might at the next shot cause a burst.

Be sure to use only low-pressure powder, if you use smokeless, as high-pressure powders are dangerous in a "break-down" action revolver. Gallery ammunition in a .38 new model solid frame Smith & Wesson revolver gives good shooting.

Many people do not understand this difference in powder pressure, and injure their revolvers by experimenting with what become practically "blasting" instead of propelling charges.

CHAPTER III

CLEANING AND CARE OF PISTOLS

ALWAYS clean your pistol the moment you have finished shooting. If you leave it over till the next day, you may as well throw it away as expect to win prizes with it.

The larger the calibre, the easier it is to clean and the less chance is there of spoiling the rifling by jamming the rod in it. I prefer wooden rods as less apt to spoil the rifling, but the very narrow calibres require a metal rod (soft metal for preference), as the wood would have to be too thin and would be liable to break in the bore.

Clean from the breech, not the muzzle end if the make permits of this; the last fraction of an inch at the muzzle is where the rifling, if damaged, spoils the shooting most. For the same reason, it is as well to have the rifling "reamed off" at the mouth of the muzzle, so that the edge of it is protected. Examine the interior of your barrel at frequent intervals after cleaning, to see if there is any damage going on from corrosion.

Use the cleaning fluids recommended for the particular powder you are using, as what may be good for one powder is of no use for another.

The great thing is to clean very thoroughly. I use cotton-wool of the best quality rather than tow, and I do not use boiling water unless in very exceptional cases, for fear of overlooking a spot in drying, and getting rust in consequence. If necessary to use water to remove fouling, let it be as hot as possible, but this cannot be done if the barrel is not capable of being separated from the action.

Do not try to oil the lock, or put it right; send it occasionally to the maker to be seen to. It is also well to have a cleaning kit with wooden not metal (except for calibres of .32 or less) cleaning rods, cotton-wool, cleaning fluids, screw-drivers, etc., all in proper compartments, and to *put them back when used*. See that the cotton-wool is absolutely dry and clean before using it. Throw away such pieces after once using. Do not use too big a piece on your rod, such as would get the latter jammed in the barrel, as you may ruin the shooting qualities of the barrel by using force to remove it. Have the cleaning rods long enough, or you may bark your knuckles.

I do not care much for detachable stocks for pistols. They only turn a pistol into an inferior carbine, and the pistol is not meant for a long-range weapon.

I also do not like the cardboard cases in which American pistols are usually packed, for permanent use; they are not strong enough and are apt to injure the sights, especially fine sights. A holster, again, is not the thing in which to keep a pistol habitually, as the sights get knocked about; if the holster is used out-of-doors it gets damp inside and rusts the weapon. Great care should always be taken to see that the holster is absolutely dry inside before placing a pistol therein. To dry the inside of a holster, make some oats very hot in a saucepan and fill the holster with them, emptying them out when cold. Some American holsters are made of india-rubber, to prevent perspiration from the body rusting the pistol, but such an one is very liable to retain dampness inside after rain. The holster which I prefer (for wearing, *not* as a pistol-case) is a cowboy holster, without any button to the flap. If you fasten the flap, you cannot get the pistol out in a hurry. A lining of rabbit fur is useful in keeping out sand or dust.

My pistol-cases are good, strong, and solid, of leather, with brass corners like gun-cases. Each case holds four, placed either side by side, each pistol in its own compartment, or, with a tray, two in the tray and two below. If you have only two pistols, they can be put in a case without this upper tray, or the tray can be used for cartridges. Under all circumstances, use a good lock,—not the sort that any key fits,—keep the case locked, and wear the key on your watch-chain, so that you are sure nobody but yourself can open the case. Keep the case in a dry place, and look at the pistols occasionally, when they are not in constant use, to see that they are not rusting.

Keep your cartridges, if not in the same case as the pistols, also locked in a good leather case. This may be fitted with compartments for various calibres and loads. The word "loaded" may with advantage be inscribed inside the lid of the pistol-cases. People then feel less encouragement to meddle with the contents.

CHAPTER IV

SIGHTS

SIGHTS are made in many forms. Some suit one man best; others another. You cannot decide which suits your individual case without trying each sort for yourself.

When you find one form which suits you, it is a pity to risk spoiling your shooting by changing to others; a beginner should never do so, as he will get into an uncertain way of taking his sights, instead of always the same, which is the only way to make reliable, consistent, shooting. Of course, all your sights may be useless if you are going to shoot in a competition, consequent on the authorities making some new rule as to "fit for rough usage"; and then you will have to shoot with whatever will pass the rules.

My patent sight has, so far, complied with every rule, and it can be used for hammering nails without sustaining damage.

The main point is to have a front sight at once easily seen, and of which you see each time the *same amount*; not sometimes more and at other times less, else you cannot keep your elevation.

Also the "U" in the back sight should have bevelled edges, so as to give a sharp edge, else it looks "woolly."

Again, if you are not able to see daylight each side of the front sight when it is in the "U," you cannot be aware that you are not covering part of the front sight on one side or the other, and, therefore, whether your aim is in horizontal axis with your barrel.

The reason I prefer a "U"- to a "V"-shaped notch in the hind sight is because in the "V" you do not see this daylight so well.

As soon as you can shoot well enough to know whether bad shots are the fault of the sighting of the revolver or of your own holding, you can sight the pistol properly for yourself; and in this way you can do the sighting much more accurately, and with greater nicety, than by taking it to a gunmaker and saying: "Alter the sights to shoot three inches higher and two to the left at twenty yards, and open the 'U' a little," etc. To do this, have front and hind sights made of horn, put in temporarily, without any "U" in the hind sight, and both hind and front sights a little higher than you think necessary. Then go to the range with your pistol and several files of various sizes, including some that are round. Make a slight "U" in the *measured* centre of the top edge of the back sight. Shoot a few shots at the range you want to sight for (taking care that you do not go clean over the top of the butt, owing to being sighted too high), and then keep working with the files, first at one sight and then at the other, till you get them approximately right.

Do not cut the "U" down too close to the barrel, as it will then give you a blurry aim, especially when the barrel gets hot. If you find you shoot too high, unless you cut this "U" down take out the front sight and put in another higher one, rather than file the "U" unduly low.

Remember when filing: Filing at the bottom of the "U" makes you shoot *lower*; filing at the top of the front sight makes you shoot *higher*; filing on the side of the "U" or the front sight makes you shoot *towards* the side on which you have filed. Therefore, by filing a very little at a time, where necessary, you can at last get your sighting perfect. Be sure to file a very little at a time, or you will overdo it. As in sculpture, you can easily take off, but cannot replace. If you have taken off too much anywhere, you may be able to correct this by filing so as to alter the direction. For instance, if you have been shooting too much to the right, you can correct this by filing on the left of the front sight or the left of the "U," whichever makes the more symmetrical job; but if, by doing so, you make the front sight too small or too narrow or make the "U" too wide, there is nothing to do but to put in a new front or hind sight and begin shooting and filing again.

When you have got the sighting perfect, work carefully with your file (taking great care not to spoil the edge of the "U" nearest to the eye when aiming), and give a chamfered or bevelled edge to the other side of the "U," so that it has a knife-edge. This is to make the "U" look clear and yet allow the back sight to be strong. On this principle, you can let the hind sight be strong and over a quarter of an inch thick, and yet have a nice, clear "U." Do not have the "U" deeper than a semicircle. If this "U" is too deep, it hampers your view of the object aimed at. In fact, it should not be quite a real "U," but a semicircle. You can also file all round the front sight, giving it a taper toward the muzzle, but keeping unaltered the silhouette that you see when aiming, so that the outline shall then stand clear to the eye.

A gunmaker's vise (padded, so as not to bruise the revolver) is a useful thing, as it leaves both your hands free to use the files.

I cannot tell you how much you may undercut the front sight, assuming you intend to use it in competition, as the rules alter so from year to year. I have an undercut bead-sight which some years was allowed at Bisley as "Military," and in other years not. The best plan, if you are in any doubt as to its passing, is to send your revolver to be passed by the committee before competing.

When you have finished, and have had a final shoot to see if this finishing has not spoilt your elevation, etc., you can send your pistol to the maker, and ask him to make your sights precisely like your model ones, and to fix them permanently on the pistol *without screws, if for Bisley use*, so as to comply with the rules. When you get the pistol with these sights, if the work has been properly done, a very little more filing will put the matter right.

Should you not be shooting at Bisley, or at any of those clubs which shoot under Bisley rules, you can, of course, get a pistol with Smith & Wesson's "Ira Paine" adjustable sights. Carry a miniature folding gilt screw-driver and sight-case on your watch-chain, as I do, and you will then be able to shoot in any light, at any range, or in any style of shooting, by merely giving a slight turn to the adjusting screws to alter your elevation or direction; or take out a sight from your little case of sights, if a sight breaks or you want a different size or shape. Public opinion has not yet been educated to the point of considering this "a practical military sight," but this will come—in time.

EXTRACTS FROM SPECIFICATIONS OF WALTER WINANS'S REVOLVER FRONT SIGHT

"Great difficulty has hitherto been experienced in seeing the same amount of front sight each time aim is taken, unless the base of the sight is sufficiently undercut to form a 'bead-sight'; such undercutting being, however, detrimental, as it weakens the 'sight' and renders it very liable to injury, and is not permissible in Bisley revolver competitions. The object of my invention is, therefore, to overcome this difficulty, and to this end I make the 'sight' of metal, horn, wood, or other hard substance, with a strong, wide base, preferably of the 'barleycorn' or triangular section.

"The face of the upper part of the 'sight' facing the marksman (as much of it as it is desirable to see in aiming) is made vertical, or inclined slightly towards the marksman, so as to cause it to appear black, as if in shadow. The visible part of the sight below the face inclines forward from the marksman, and downward, so as to reflect the light and enable the face of the sight to be at once distinguished by its difference of shade from the lower part. It may be polished or plated to assist in reflecting the light, while as a contrast, the vertical face is cross-filed, or 'roughed,' or may be hollowed out so as to be in shadow, and give it a 'dead' black appearance.

"In the drawing, I have shown what I consider the best means of carrying this out. Fig. 1 is a side view, full size, of a portion of a revolver barrel fitted with my improved 'front sight.'

"Fig. 2 and Fig. 3 are sections of the barrel at A B, showing two forms which the sight may assume in section, one having straight sides, the other concave. I show in Figs. 4 and 4*, on a larger scale, for the sake of clearness, a side and plan view of the sight shown in Fig. 1, and in Fig. 5 a modification of this shape. Figs. 6 and 7 are end views, showing two sectional forms of the sight, and corresponding in size with Figs. 4 and 5. In Figs. 1 and 4, it will be seen that *a* is the vertical face of the sight, which is designed to present a dark appearance to the marksman; and *b* is the polished, inclined surface, which takes a rounded form. In the modification, Fig. 5, the face *a* is slightly inclined towards the marksman, and the bright or polished surface *b* takes the form of a flat incline."

CHAPTER V

LEARNING TO SHOOT

IT is assumed that you have procured an accurate pistol, properly sighted. It is best to use a single-shot pistol or revolver as an automatic pistol cannot well be used as a single loader and for a beginner is very dangerous with the magazine charged.

First, make sure that it is unloaded. *Always* do this before handling a pistol.

Take a bottle of sight-black and paint both sights over with the liquid. I have seen men try to compete, with their sights in a shiny state, which made it impossible for them to make good shooting on a white target with black "bull."

For game shooting, or for military purposes, of course, a "dead" white (ivory for choice) tip to the front sight is preferable, or my patent military front sight, which answers the purposes both of a light on dark, or dark on light sight.

With a pistol the first thing to consider is safety. It is, owing to its shortness, one of the most dangerous of firearms to handle. Even an expert must exercise great care; and in the hands of a beginner or a careless person it may be fearfully dangerous. I have had many very narrow escapes in teaching men how to shoot; it is not even safe to be behind them; they will turn round with the pistol at full-cock, pointing it at you, and say: "I cannot understand why it will not go off; see! I am pulling as hard as I can at the trigger."

It is indispensable to have a safe background. Some people think that if the target is fastened to the trunk of a tree it is all safe, since the bullet will not go through the tree. This may be so if the tree is hit, but the bullet will, most likely, go past the tree when the beginner fires; or, what is just as dangerous, graze the tree and go off at an angle. Also, in shooting with round bullets, and light gallery ammunition, the bullets may rebound from a hard tree and come back on the shooter. This I have actually seen happen.

A good background is a high sandy bank, a thick pile of fagots, or, if not closer than fifty yards, a high brick or stone wall. The target may be stood some fifteen yards away from the wall to prevent danger of a bullet coming back on the shooter, and then the shooter can be far enough from the wall, if the wall is a background. If a lot of shooting is done, it is not very good for the wall, and if many shots hit the same spot they may gradually make a hole. Iron butts are expensive, especially for the large surface required by a beginner; at twenty yards, a beginner could not in my opinion safely shoot at a background less than twelve feet high and some ten in width. Even then there should not be any one beyond it within half a mile, lest he should happen to let off by accident. Shooting out to sea is safe, if one keeps a good lookout for boats; but the glare from the water is bad. A sand or chalk pit is a good place to shoot in, or one can shoot against a high chalk cliff. It is dangerous to shoot anywhere where people cross unexpectedly, as from round the corner of a building.

The great thing is that *the pistol should never point in any direction where it would matter if it went off by accident.* This rule should be observed even with an empty pistol, because so many "I-did-not-know-it-was-loaded" accidents occur.

Having got a butt, the learner should take a firm, narrow wooden table and place it some ten yards from the target. This target is preferably a "Bisley fifty-yards target," four-inch bull's-eye. The Bisley cardboard targets are cheap; and, by pasting white patches on the white and black on the bull's-eye bullet-holes, one target can be used for a long time. I refer to the fifty-yards target because this four-inch bull's-eye is very easy to hit at ten yards' range. The Bisley revolver "bull's-eyes" count, at all ranges, seven points; the concentric rings counting one point less, each, till the outermost one, which counts two points. The highest possible score, therefore, for the six shots is forty-two, or six times seven. It is best to shoot at this very big "bull" at ten yards, as making "bull's-eyes" encourages the beginner; and, as he gets more proficient, the two-inch twenty yards "bull" can be substituted. This I think preferable to going back farther from the target as your skill increases; also it is safer, for the nearer the shooter is to the butt the wider his shots would have to be for him to miss it; whereas, if he goes back to fifty yards he may easily shoot over a very high butt.

Place your empty pistol on the table, the weapon lying on its left side with the muzzle towards the target. The table is preferably a narrow one, so that, during the process of loading, the muzzle points to the ground beyond the table and not to the table itself, an accidental discharge being thus immaterial; a foot wide is about right; the length does not matter, so long as it will hold your field-glasses, cleaning things, and cartridges.

POSITION.—The position for shooting which I am now going to describe, is the one in which I shoot and the one which I have found from experience suits me best. This position, however, will have to be modified according to the build of the shooter; a stouter or shorter-necked man than myself might have to stand more sideways.

Stand facing the target; the right foot pointing straight for the target, or perhaps a shade to the left (if the ground is slippery, this gives you a firmer foothold); the left heel distant from six to nine inches to the left of the right foot, according to your height (my distance is eight inches), and about an inch farther back; the feet turned out about as much as is natural to you when standing.

Stand perfectly upright, not craning your head forward; the left arm should hang down straight and close to the side in the position of "Attention." Some people bend the left arm and rest the hand on the hip; but I think this looks affected, and it is not as workmanlike as if the arm hangs straight down.

If you are trying to "hold" an especially important shot, and find yourself wobbling off your aim, it is a great help to grip your thigh hard with your left hand; this especially applies in a gusty wind.

Now lift the pistol with your right hand (the weapon is empty, remember) and cock it. There are two ways of cocking: one using both hands and one using only the shooting hand. I do not refer to the double-action revolver cocked by pulling back the trigger, as I do not think shooting with much accuracy can be done by this method; and it is, moreover, the cause of half the accidents happening with the "I-did-not-know-it-was-loaded" shooters. The cocking by the trigger is only useful in a revolver for self-defence at very close quarters.

To return, this single-handed cocking is done by putting the thumb on the hammer and by the action of the thumb muscles alone bring it to full-cock. Take particular care that the first finger is clear of the trigger, or else you will either break or injure the sear notch, or have an accidental "let-off." With practice, this way of cocking becomes very easy, and can be done with great rapidity. I personally can also let the pistol down to half-cock (manipulating the pistol with one hand, with the trigger finger and thumb); but I would not advise a beginner to try this, except with an empty pistol and even then only one that he does not mind the chance of spoiling, as he is very apt to break the nose of the sear if he bungles it.

By practice, the thumb and forefinger muscles (*abductor pollicis* and *adductor indicis*) develop enormously, and you need not mind if at first it seems difficult; but stop at first as soon as they feel tired, or you may strain them. Pistol-shooting is good also for the flexors of the forearm and for the dorsal muscles. A small hammer with short "fall" is easiest to cock, as well as to make good shooting with, for such a hammer takes less time in falling, and the aim is, in consequence, less likely to be disturbed.

The beginner will find that it assists the cocking to give the pistol a slight tilt to the right and upwards, taking great care to bring it back with the hind-sight *horizontal* afterwards, as holding the sights tilted is one of the chief causes of bad shooting.

For double-handed cocking, assist the right hand by taking the pistol barrel in the left hand; keep the barrel horizontal and pointed at the target, *not* towards your left-hand neighbour (if you are competing), as is often done; and, while it is thus steadied, cock gently, not with a jerk, bringing the hammer well beyond full-cock, so that it sinks back into the bent with a well-defined click, keeping the first finger clear of the trigger.

Now, stand with the pistol in your right hand, just clear of the table; right arm full stretch. The first finger must be outside the trigger-guard (*not touching the trigger*) during this stage.

Some Englishmen shoot with the second finger on the trigger and the first along the pistol; but this is a clumsy way, and the first finger is apt to be burnt with the escape of gas from the cylinder, if a revolver is used. The habit was acquired from shooting the Martini rifle, the clumsy "grip" of which made this manner of holding necessary.

The great thing is to have your grip *as high as you can* on the stock, in line with the axis of the barrel, or as near this as is practicable. With the Smith & Wesson Russian Model (now no longer manufactured) I have it actually in line with the bore of the barrel.

Some pistols for the British market often have specially long, big handles, or stocks, because of the habit (or is it the Regulation Position?) of holding the stock low down with the little finger beneath, prevalent in England. Now this sort of position makes the recoil come at an angle to the wrist, throws the barrel up at the recoil, spoiling the accuracy, and puts more strain on the wrist than is necessary. I remember a very strong-wristed man firing one of my heavily charged fifty-yards revolvers and spraining his wrist at the first shot, owing to holding it in this way; whilst I have fired hundreds of rapid-firing shots straight on end with it without hurting myself. I take the recoil just as a man catches a hard-thrown ball, letting arm, hand, and wrist fly up together.

The pistol barrel, hand, and arm should all be nearly in one line, the thumb along the left side, so as to prevent jerking to the left in pressing the trigger (in the same way as the left arm is fully extended in shooting with the shotgun), and not crooked, as all beginners insist on holding it.

You must be constantly on the watch that you do not crook your thumb, until the extended position becomes second nature to you. Some makes of pistols, however, have the extractor lever in a position which renders this grip with extended thumb impossible.

For the benefit of beginners who are not target rifle-shots, the following explanation may be necessary: The target, for the convenience of locating shot-holes, is supposed to represent the face of a clock. The top of the bull's-eye (which we term "bull" for brevity) is called XII o'clock, as that is, of course, where the numeral XII appears on a clock face, and so on for all the other numerals: half-past four, for instance, is half-way between where the numerals IV and V appear on a clock. I was once shooting in the presence of a foreign naval officer, and when I made a "half-past five" "bull" shot he said, "South-east," his professional instinct making him liken the target to the face of a compass.

First take a deep breath, and fill your lungs. Now slowly bring your right arm to the horizontal, keeping your eyes fixed on the bottom edge—at "six o'clock"—of the "bull"; whilst you are doing this, put your forefinger inside the trigger-guard, and gradually begin to feel the trigger and steadily increase the pressure on it *straight back, not sideways*. Whilst you are doing all this, also gradually stiffen all your muscles so that you are braced up, especially about the right shoulder, as though you were walking along the pavement and saw a man coming towards you whom you meant to shoulder out of your path.

You may breathe naturally until the pistol is levelled, then hold your breath; if you cannot get your aim satisfactorily before you feel you want to take a fresh breath, lower the pistol, take a deep breath, and try again. If you have followed these directions carefully, you will find, when the hind sight comes to the level of your eyes (closing your left eye or not, as you find best, without any lowering of the head), the front sight will be seen through the middle of the "U" pointed at the bottom of the bull's-eye, the top of the front sight just touching it at "six o'clock." If everything has been done perfectly, at the moment this occurs the pressure on the trigger will have been increased sufficiently to cause the hammer to fall, and, after it has fallen, you will see the top of the front sight *still* just touching the bull's-eye at its bottom edge.

If the pistol had been loaded (assuming, of course, that it was an accurate shooting one and properly sighted), you would have had a central bull's-eye for your shot. Most likely, however, you will find that the pistol came up all of a tremble, and that, as the hammer fell, the front sight was jerked very wide of the "bull" and perhaps even hidden by the hind sight.

Do not be discouraged, but cock and try again. By the way, it is best to use a "dummy" cartridge or an exploded one whilst doing this "snapping" practice, as otherwise the jar may do damage to the plunger and perhaps break the mainspring. There are dummy cartridges, made with a rubber "buffer," for this practice.

If you still find your hand shaky (and it is not naturally so), it most probably arises from your gripping too hard.

The action of "letting off" should be like squeezing an orange—a squeeze of the *whole hand*. Start with a light grip when your hand is down, and gradually squeeze as you come up, the trigger-finger squeezing *back*; and the hammer will fall without the least tremor or without the sights moving off the point they covered during the fall of the hammer. The main thing of all in pistol shooting is to *squeeze straight back*. Whenever you find yourself shooting badly see if you are not "*pulling off to one side*"; and in nine cases out of ten you will discover that this was the cause of your bad shooting.

Some men can never squeeze the trigger straight back, and have to allow for this by getting the hind sight "set over" to one side to correct it; but this is a slovenly way of shooting, and, as the pull to one side may vary according to the "jumpiness" of the shooter, it prevents his being a really first-class shot.

Keep the hind sight perfectly horizontal; beginners are prone to cant it on one side, which puts the bullet to the side towards which you cant.

After a little practice, you will be able to "call" your shots, that is to say, you will be able, the moment the cartridge explodes, to say where the shot has struck the target, as you know where the sights were pointed at the "squeeze-off."

After six shots, make a pencil-cross over each bullet-hole, so as to know where your former shots hit. After twelve hits it is best to take a fresh target. At the end of the day's shooting, you can cover the holes by pasting black patches on the bull's-eye holes and white on the rest, and use the target again.

I will now say why I insist upon the importance of a table being before the shooter. The usual procedure for a beginner with the pistol is this: He cocks the pistol with both hands, pointing it at the spectators on his left whilst doing so; he then holds it with his right arm close to his side, pointing it to the ground at his right foot. He then brings it up with a flourish, high above his head, and lowers it to the target, jerks the trigger, and "looses off." Of course he does not hit the target, but makes a very wild shot. After a few more shots on this principle, getting more and more wild, and making bigger flourishes with his pistol, he finally lets it off by accident whilst his arm is hanging by his side; and he is lucky if he does not make a hole in his right foot.

I remember once a man telling me (he professed to be an expert with the revolver) that I was wrong in keeping my revolver pointed in front of me towards the target when preparing to shoot. "You ought to hold it like this," he said, letting his right arm hang close to his side and keeping the revolver pointing downwards; "then it is quite safe." At that moment it went off and blew a big hole in the ground within an inch of his foot!

By my system of having a table in front of the shooter, close to which he stands, and from which he lifts the pistol, he cannot shoot down into his feet. But he must never turn round or leave the table without first unloading the pistol and placing it on the table; nor, on any account, must he let any one go up to the target or be in front or even get level with him whilst the pistol is in his hand.

Now, as to the trick of lifting the pistol above one's head before firing: I cannot understand why people want to do this. It only frightens spectators; besides, the shooter is running the risk of shooting himself through the head; and in competitions or in self-defence time is too valuable to waste in such antics.

When you are pretty confident that you can keep your sights properly aligned at the bottom edge of the "bull" while the hammer is falling, you can try a few shots with a loaded pistol. It is best to load only some of the chambers, if using a revolver, irregularly spin the cylinder round, after the revolver is closed and at half-cock, so as not to know which chambers are loaded, and every time you find you jerk off with a shot, return to the snapping-empty-cartridge practice. This latter is good practice, even when you become a skilled shot.

Place the box of cartridges beside, and to the right of, the pistol. Use only a very small charge (gallery ammunition for choice) at first, as nothing puts a beginner off so much as the fear of recoil. Stand behind the table, the pistol being between you and the target, and take the pistol by its stock in the right hand. Do not turn the muzzle to the left, but straight out towards the target. Put it in your left hand and load it. This procedure varies with different makes of revolvers; with the Smith & Wesson, Russian, and Winans models, you lift the catch with your left thumb and press the barrel down with the same hand till it (the barrel) is perpendicular, pointing to the ground. But whatever the mechanism, when the pistol is open for loading, the barrel should be pointing downwards, yet in line for the target.

If a cartridge projects too much, remove it, as it is dangerous and may explode prematurely from friction against the breech of the revolver. In loading, of course have the pistol at half-, not full-cock. Close it by elevating the breech with the right hand, not by raising the barrel with the left, as in the latter case the cartridges may drop out. This rule applies also to the hand ejecting revolvers. See that the snap, or other fastening, is properly closed. If your shot goes wide of the bull, be sure, before you alter your aim for the next shot, whether it is not your "squeeze-off" which is wrong.

A practised shot can correct the shooting of his pistol by "aiming-off" enough to rectify any error in sights. But the beginner had better not attempt this: he will find enough to do in trying to hold straight under the bull.

Do not mind if your score does not *"count"* much; those who do not understand shooting judge the goodness of a score by how much it counts, or by how many shots are in or near the bull's-eye. In reality, it is the *group* which constitutes a good score. One score may consist of the highest possible,—forty-two points (all six shots bull's-eyes),—and another may only count twelve points; and yet the latter may be far the better "shoot."

I will explain: In the first case, the shots may be "all round" the bull, "nicking" the edges; they would require, therefore, a circle of more than four inches (on the target you are at present shooting at) to cover them. The other score may consist of all six bullet-holes cutting into each other at an extreme edge of the target, but making a group which could be covered with a postage-stamp. The first "shoot" is a wild, bad score for ten yards' range at a four-inch bull, although it counts the highest possible in conventional scoring. The other is a magnificent shoot, that any one might be proud of; the fact of its being up in the corner merely showing that the sights were wrong, not the shooter's "holding." A few touches of the file, or knocking sideways the hind sight, will put this error right. Never mind, therefore, about scoring many points; merely shoot for *group*. You will gradually find your groups getting smaller and smaller as you improve; it is then merely a matter of filing to get good scoring.

As your four-inch bull's-eye is too large for real shooting at ten yards, you must remember that the sighting of the pistol should put the bullets *one inch only into* this size bull at "VI o'clock," not into the middle of it. The reason is that, practically, the trajectory of a pistol is the same at twenty as at ten yards; and as the English regulation bull at twenty yards is two inches, you want the twenty-yards sighted pistol to put the shots into the centre of the two-inch bull when you aim at the bottom edge. In other words, you want it to shoot an inch higher than your aim at that distance. Therefore, if with your four-inch bull, aiming at the bottom edge, you go into the bull one inch up, it means a central bull's-eye shot on a two-inch bull. The reason I recommend aiming at the bottom of the bull's-eye instead of at the middle of it is that if you try to put a black bead in the middle of a black bull's-eye, you cannot see either properly; if you whiten the bead of the fore sight, then you cannot see it clearly against the white of the target in "coming up" to a bull. Nobody can hold *absolutely* steady on the "bull" for more than a fraction of a second; you have to "come up" from below and "squeeze off" as you get your sights aligned.

It is best to have your cleaning appliances on the table, or otherwise handy, when shooting, and every now and again to have a look through the barrel and a wipe-out; you might otherwise be inclined to attribute to bad shooting what may be caused by leading or hard fouling in the barrel. I have a little cupboard under my table with a lock and key, in which I keep my cleaning apparatus, cartridges, etc. (but *not* the pistol), to save the trouble of carrying them to the range.

Always clean a pistol as soon after shooting as possible, and clean very thoroughly.

For real work, I prefer a pistol when it is half worn out, as everything then works smoothly and there is less danger of jambing. Rust in the rifling may entirely spoil accuracy, as, if you work it off, the bore gets enlarged and the bullets "strip." I never like to compete with a perfectly new pistol; all pistols have their peculiarities, and it is necessary to get used to one, to "break it in," before trusting it to obey one's slightest hint.

It is sometimes useful to be able to shoot with the left hand; as, for instance, if the right hand is disabled, the right arm held, etc., and for an officer with a sword in his right hand. If the novice has resolution enough to divide his practising, *from the beginning*, between both hands, he will be able to shoot nearly as well with his "left" hand as with his right. I have put quotation marks round "left" as I mean by this the hand not usually employed; a left-handed man's right hand being in this sense his "left."

I have also noticed that a left-handed man can shoot more evenly with both hands; that is to say, he is not much better or worse with either hand, not being so helpless with his right hand as a normally handed man is with his left. In all the directions for shooting, for left-handed work merely change "right leg" to "left leg"; "right arm" to "left arm," etc.

CHAPTER VI

RAPID FIRING

RAPID firing, in my opinion, is the most practical style of shooting; a pistol is not a weapon for deliberate shooting, but for lightning rapidity at short range.

If you are using a revolver it is necessary to get one which works as loosely and as easily as possible. A half-worn-out revolver is best, as it works freer. Next, file the mainspring as weak as it is possible to have it without risk of too many misfires. If it has one misfire in every twenty shots, or so, it does not matter, the great thing being to have it cock easily. An automatic pistol is the weapon for this, a revolver being quite out of date. A very big front sight and a big "U" in the back one are advisable.

As the target rises, "come up," quickly, increasing the pressure on the trigger as you "come up," so that the pistol goes off the moment it is horizontal and the sights are *about* right. I say *about* because there is not time to correct the aim.

Be sure to *squeeze back*—not jerk off. It is possible, with practice, to get this "snap shot" into the "bull" or touching it. As this first shot goes off, *be especially careful to take all pressure off the trigger*. Unless you are very careful you will keep a slight pressure on the trigger with your first finger, and if you are using an automatic the next shot will go off before you mean it to.

Your right arm—and in fact, the whole of your body—should be immovable. Your aim at each shot ought not to be disturbed enough to be more than a few inches off the "bull."

After each shot begin a steadily increasing pressure *straight back*, and *without a jerk*, trying at the same time to get your sights as near the "bull" as you can before the pistol goes off again. You can fire as quickly as you can get your aim.

If using an automatic pistol, all that you have to do is to *release the pressure on the trigger the moment each shot goes off*, and *instantly* begin to squeeze again as you get your next aim. Do not keep on too long; half a dozen practice scores are ample at a time. One only gets erratic and wild if one continues too long, and the pistol also gets hot.

The sighting may have to be different in this from that required for slower shooting. Some men shoot up in one corner when snap-shooting with the heavy trigger-pull of the automatic pistol; and it is preferable to have the sighting so that one can aim straight under the "bull," instead of having to make allowance for the jerking off. The trigger-pull should be as light as is deemed compatible with safety, but the automatic pistols so far on the market have a very heavy trigger-pull.

Wearing glasses to protect the eyes against half-burnt powder fumes is very important in shooting an automatic.

CHAPTER VII

TRAVERSING TARGET

Target Moving Across the Line of Fire at Twenty Yards

THIS is not so difficult as rapid-firing. The chief difficulty is that when your aim is right horizontally, you may be wrong vertically, and *vice versa*.

When first practising, have a target made with a black band two inches wide running down the middle of the target, instead of the usual bull's-eye. Begin your practice at this, having it first put up with the black band vertical, and then with it horizontal. Shooting at it vertical will show you if you are getting the right allowance in front in your aim. When it is horizontal, it will show you if your elevation is correct. This can be elaborated by having black bands painted or pasted on the back of an ordinary target, and, with its back towards you, shooting at them. Then, by turning it over after the six shots have been fired, you will see what score you would have made on a regulation target. The reason for this practice is that there are two things to attend to. One is the "*allowance*" *in front*, the other is the "*elevation*"; and if a beginner tries to think of both at once, it will confuse him.

If, after you have got pretty certain of your "allowance," you go to "elevation," you will most likely lose your "allowance," and have to go back to the vertical band; and so on, alternately, till you can trust yourself at the regulation bull.

Most people, unless they use alternate hands, find the "run" one way easier than the other.

I prefer higher elevation in sights for this competition. Instead of aiming to touch the "bull" at "VI o'clock" to get a central "bull," the aim should be at the actual elevation you want the bullet to go, so as to enable you to aim off at "III o'clock" and "IX o'clock" for right and left runs respectively.

Some people who are slower on the trigger—that is, who take longer to give the order to the trigger-finger when their eye says the aim is right—may need more allowance.

There is in astronomical work a technical term ("reaction time") for the process of timing first contact in eclipses, and each observer deducts his own personal error, which seems constant to him. This allowance varies in revolver shooting with different men.

Some men aim at a spot, and wait for the target to come up to it; but this is useless, as any one knows who has shot moving game with a gun.

Stand absolutely square to the front, or perhaps a little more toward the side on which you find it most difficult to follow the target. Plant the feet slightly farther apart than for other competitions, *and swing the whole of the upper part of the body from the hips*. Do *not* swing your right arm, keeping the rest of the body still. The shoulder-joint does not give so smooth a horizontal swing as swinging from the hips. Moreover, if you swing the arm, you have to turn the head, or else have to look out of the corners of your eyes, instead of straight before you.

Let the whole of the upper part of your body be held rigid, and swing only on the hips. Lift your pistol from the table as the target appears, and swing with the target, bringing up the pistol on a diagonal line (this is the resultant of the vertical rise from the shoulder and the horizontal swing of the hips). Let the sights come horizontal to the eyes a little in front of the proposed allowance; and, as you keep your arm moving in front of the bull, gradually let the bull *overtake you*, till it is the right allowance behind your sight; and *still keep on swinging*. All this time be gradually squeezing the trigger, so that it squeezes off just when the aim is right. *Be sure not to stop swinging before the pistol goes off*.

I do not think there is any advantage in keeping your arm up between runs of the target; it tires the arm, and you cannot make the diagonal swing up to your spot in front of the bull.

I do not think it is of any use deciding to fire upon a certain part of the "run": it is best to fire when you feel you are aiming right, and you may get this feeling sooner in the "run" on some days than on others.

There is a tendency to "follow" too long, and then, owing to lack of time, to jerk off just as the target disappears. I have made "bulls" when the target was almost out of sight, in fact, I did so in my record shoot, at Bisley, where there used to be such a competition: but this is a bad habit to contract, and a risky sort of shot, as it is almost sure to be too far behind, or even to be fired into the shield in front of the target; though, of course, if you have not a good aim, it is better to delay as long as possible, rather than to shoot earlier with a bad aim.

Be sure in your range that your shield is bulletproof, or you may get into the habit of making "bulls" when the target is "sitting" behind the shield, by shooting through it. To economize space, you can have this target run in front of your disappearing-target apparatus, putting the latter out of the way when not needed; this latter will also serve for stationary-target purposes, and to hold the fifty-yards target. Do not have a target which runs by gravitation, as shooting at a target which is running downhill requires quite different sighting from that needed with one running horizontally.

CHAPTER VIII

GALLERY SHOOTING

A PRIVATE gallery can easily be fitted up in the cellars of large country, or even town, houses. All that is needed is a gallery of a certain length—ten yards will suffice at a pinch, with the targets and butt (such as I describe in the chapter on Stage Shooting) at one end. The targets should be lighted from above, preferably by a skylight in the daytime, and by gas, lamp, or electric light at night. When artificial light is used, it should be screened, so that from the firing-point the targets are distinct, but the source of light invisible. At the firing-point it is difficult to get a satisfactory light. If this gallery is not made in a greenhouse, which, of course, would give ample light to sight by in the day, I think there is no use in trying to get the light to shine on your sights. If it is behind you, you stand in your own light. If enough above you to prevent this, the light only shines on the top edges of your sights, and is thus worse than useless. I find it best to have enough light behind you to enable you to load by, and to trust to seeing the sights in a black silhouette against the target. You may, for this reason, have to alter your sights from the elevation which suits you out-of-doors.

You should have a ventilating shaft straight above the muzzle of your pistol, and, if possible, a fan to draw off the fumes and smoke; one worked by electricity or water-power is best.

It is expedient to use only the lightest gallery ammunition, and it deadens the sound if you have the walls covered with some material hung loosely. Boiler-felt is very good for the purpose. Also, if you shoot through a hole in a partition screen, it helps to deaden the sound.

I prefer a big-calibre pistol in competition, as it gives a better chance to score; a shot which would be just out of the bull with a small bullet, may just cut the bull with a large ball. The bullet-hole is also more easily seen, but the bullet must be spherical, or you will have to use too heavy a charge of powder to propel it.

The self-registering targets, such as are used for miniature .22 calibre rifles, I do not find very satisfactory; the larger size of the bullet makes it liable to strike two compartments at the same time, giving you a double score, and the impact of the bullet is, moreover, too heavy for the mechanism. I prefer card targets or the Gastinne Renette target which registers hits at the firing-point.

On no account have targets that necessitate any one's going down the range, or coming out from a mantlet, to change. There is sure to be an accident sooner or later. Have them made to draw up to the firing-point for examination and change, and never let any one turn round with a pistol in his hand. In fact, observe all the rules as to table to fire from, etc., which I give in the chapter on Learning to Shoot. All these rules apply equally to gallery shooting.

As the gallery is generally narrow, it will be difficult to have traversing targets, but you can have the Bisley targets.

Such a gallery will be an endless source of amusement in the winter evenings, after dinner; and the ladies can shoot as well as the men.

It is advisable to handicap the good shots, so as to give all an equal chance.

Gallery shooting is by far the most scientific style of pistol-shooting, if you use a very light load, fine sights, and hair-trigger; therefore you can have smaller bull's-eyes and subdivisions than the Bisley ones. The American and French targets are better subdivided for this purpose. Messrs. De La Rue make me special "ace of hearts" packs of cards for use as targets. For experimental work also, a gallery is much more reliable than shooting out-of-doors.

When shooting gallery ammunition in which the bullets are "seated" low down, it is best to have a groove line impressed in the cartridge shell to prevent the bullet working up; if you have not got this impression in the shell, look into the cartridges before putting them into the chambers, as a bullet may have worked itself up, which would cause a weak, low shot. Push the bullet down with a loading rod, or pencil, before you insert the cartridge into the chamber, if you find it shifted. Also, if, after firing a few shots from a revolver with this ammunition, you, for any cause, stop and want to re-load the chambers which have been fired, it is as well to take out all the cartridges that have not been fired and examine them, as the jar of firing may have started some of the bullets.

CHAPTER IX

TWENTY YARDS STATIONARY TARGET

I HAVE already described how to stand and shoot at a stationary target. There are a few points to be observed, however, which specially apply to this range when shooting at Bisley. Before competing at any one of the limited-entry competitions, it is well to be sure that you are shooting up to your proper form, as mistakes cannot be corrected after once commencing.

Personally I think it best (if shooting every day or most of the ten days) not to enter in a limited-entry competition till after the first two days of the meeting, as one gets steadied down by then and grows more accustomed to the surroundings.

As sighting varies from day to day, and even from hour to hour, it may be as well to have a pool shoot for sighting purposes first; but I personally never do so, as I think it is a pity to chance wasting a good score in pool. The moment you have "found the spot," leave off pool; do not stop to finish a score.

I prefer doing my sighting on an "unlimited-entry" competition ticket, so that in case I make a "highest possible," that score is not wasted.

The early morning, from 9 till 11 A.M., is the best time for shooting; and then, perhaps, late in the evening. One should watch for a good time when the light is favourable; often the wind will drop late in the evening, half an hour before "gunfire," after blowing hard all day.

There is often a good light after rain. I rather like shooting in the rain, and have made some of my best shots in it. The light is then good; and there is then no glare on the target; bullets make very big, ragged holes on a wet target; and sometimes a shot which would not cut the bull on a dry target may do so on a wet one, owing to its making a larger hole.[1] The flat-topped bullets make very big, "clean" holes.

If you have a target with a doubtful shot, that is to say, one for which you think you are entitled to a higher count than the range officer gives you, do not touch it, or thrust anything (your finger or a pencil) into the hole to demonstrate that the shot cuts into the bull's-eye or the line you claim. If you push anything into the hole you will spoil its outline and destroy all evidence of the point at which the bullet had cut. In doubtful cases, the range officer puts a bullet of the same calibre (which has been pushed with a rod through a revolver barrel previously) into the hole, and examines it whilst in this position with a magnifying-glass.

Accept the range officer's decision as final; *never* "protest" a decision of his.

Look at the target through your glass and see that it has no bullet-holes in it before you begin to shoot; and refuse to shoot at a patched target, except at pool. A patch may fall off a shot made by a previous competitor and confuse your score, besides making the target indistinct and throwing doubt on a record score by you if you should happen to make one on such a target. Also see that the bull's-eye is black; some are badly printed, and the "bull" is grey and indistinct.

Shoot very slowly and deliberately. There is no hurry. The time limit of two minutes would be ample within which to fire twenty-four shots—and you have only to fire six.

If you are dissatisfied with your aim, or your arm is getting tired, or a gust of wind comes, put the revolver down without firing. Look down on the grass to rest your eyes, and wipe your hands; a little sawdust is a good thing to rub them with on hot days.

When it is gusty, putting up the pistol just as you think a lull is coming, instead of waiting *for* the lull, gives you a better chance of being "up" when the lull does come, and you can then "snap" the shot before the next gust.

If you *have* to shoot in a very high wind—as in a match, or in shooting off a tie—it is best to "snap" your shots (see chapter on Rapid Firing) and not try to hold against the wind.

If a shot strikes a little too high, or too low, or too much to either side, aim "off" the "bull" the next shot to correct it.

Do not keep altering the amount you see of your front sight if you hit too high or too low; you will never make a good score in that way. If you are out half an inch at "X o'clock," aim your next shot at half an inch off "V o'clock"; if you hit half an inch above the bull at "XII o'clock," aim half an inch below "VI o'clock" with your next shot; do not take a "coarser" sight. This is where a practical shot has the advantage over a mere "target shot."

If a shot is in the "bull" (I will assume you can easily see shots in, or partly in, the "white" at twenty yards; I can see them at fifty), and you are not sure of its exact locality, examine it with your glass.

If you are "holding" exceptionally steady, and have shot well into the "bull," though not actually central, do not aim differently to try to get the actual centre with the next shot; as a rule, if you are anything more than half in the "bull," it is better to let well alone and "hold" the same as before. I remember on one occasion I had five shots in one ragged hole at "V o'clock" in the "bull" on the sliding target; and for fear lest I should put my last shot through the same hole and have it counted as a miss, I tried to hit the "bull" at "IX o'clock" clear of that hole, and got just out of the bull.

If you have several bullets in one ragged hole, it is advisable, if there be time, to draw the range officer's attention to this before you fire the next shot, so that in case you go into the same hole or group again, he may record it and not think it a miss. If he watches the target whilst you shoot, through his glasses, he will see where your bullet goes, even if you do go into this group.

At the stationary targets, *and at those only*, it is advisable to use both hands in cocking. In cocking, if using a revolver, if there is not a distinct click, or if the action feels "woolly" or soft, put it back at half-cock, and open the revolver and see what is the matter. Most likely a bit of fouling, or piece of metal from a cartridge or bullet, or a cartridge with too thick a head or protruding cap, is the cause.

When the revolver is at full-cock, take the cylinder between the forefinger and thumb of the left hand, still holding the stock in the right hand and keeping the muzzle towards the target, and gently try to revolve the cylinder towards the right. This, at least, is the normal direction, though some makes revolve to the left. You will, perhaps, once in a dozen times, find that it goes over an appreciable amount till it locks.

Any revolver, even the best, may sometimes not bring the cylinder round quite true to the barrel; and if it does not coincide, the shot will not be accurate, owing to the bullet not going into the barrel true, and thus getting a small shaving taken off its side. A bit of fouling, metal from cartridges or bullet, "proud cap," or thick cartridge-head may cause this. By attending to the cocking in the elaborate way I have indicated, this cause of inaccuracy is avoided. (This is very important in cases where a miss would be dangerous: as when shooting objects off someone's head, or those which are held in the hand or mouth, or for the last shot on which everything depends in a match or a record score.) Also every time you open the revolver, look to see whether the caps have been hit absolutely true in the centre.

By my way of cocking, even if the revolver is not acting quite perfectly, the chambers ought to come true. If they do not, clean them very carefully. If, in spite of this, the caps are still hit on the side, it is useless to continue with that revolver until the maker has put it right.

Shoot with the smallest charge, lightest bullet, and largest calibre the rules allow, as it is easier to shoot with a small than with a "kicking" charge, and the bullet of larger calibre is more apt to cut into the bull. (This applies to all competitions at ranges not over twenty yards; beyond that distance, a big charge is more accurate. See chapter on Fifty-Yards Target.)

I do not like too small a front sight. I think that one which, in aiming, you see easily is the best. The semicircular "U" of the hind sight should be wide enough to enable you to see all round the bead of the front sight.

In pistol-shooting, the chief difficulty is in "holding" and "squeezing off" without disturbing your aim. There is no need to strain your eyes with a microscopic front sight and it makes you slow and every fraction of a second is valuable in practical shooting.

Another fault of too fine a front sight is that it is liable to get bent, just enough to spoil your aim, yet not enough to be noticeable until too late. If you try to straighten it, the odds are that you break it off and then have to waste a day or more getting another fixed, which, most likely, does not suit when done.

I always have my Bisley sights made solid with the revolver, without any screws, and have some made to shoot higher, others lower, each on a separate revolver. If I find that the light, or my shooting, does not suit one sort of sight, I take another revolver. I have some fifteen revolvers prepared in this way.

The permission to have a hind sight adjustable by being hammered to one side is worse than useless. The sight works loose, gets knocked askew, and when you begin shooting you find it is constantly shifting and spoiling your shooting. I do not call it by any means a practical military sight. If you only have one pistol have it with my front sight, sighted to your normal or average shooting, at twenty or fifty yards, to whichever you decide to confine yourself, and both back and front sights made fixtures.

Wear nailed boots, or those with corrugated rubber soles, so as not to slip. The rubber, however, is rather apt to get cut in standing on spent cartridges. A broad-brimmed cowboy hat, or sombrero, is the best headgear, except in a wind, as it keeps the glare off your eyes. I took to using these years ago, and now I see them in use by nearly all shooting men, as well as in the English army, though (unlike in the U. S. army) often rendered less serviceable by having the brim looped up on one side. I keep some of various widths of brim, and use the one most suitable for the occasion. Also a Swedish leather jacket is very good when it gets chilly, as it is very light and does not hamper your right arm as a heavier coat would do. If you do not possess one, an extra waistcoat will serve, as this will leave your arm free. An overcoat or mackintosh hampers your right arm. You are freer in a flannel shirt with turn-down collar, loose round the wrists, and no braces. A silk handkerchief tied loosely round the neck, cowboy fashion, keeps the sun off the nape of your neck.

CHAPTER X

DISAPPEARING TARGET

THIS target, which has the two-inch bull's-eye, like the twenty yards stationary target, appears and disappears at intervals of three seconds—three seconds in sight and three seconds invisible—and is shot at from a distance of twenty yards.

The rules forbid the pistol being raised from the firing-table before the target appears; and it must be lowered to the table after each shot.

Shooting in this competition is the groundwork of all the competitions other than at stationary targets; so I shall go very fully into the way of becoming proficient at this, as the other competitions should then come comparatively easy.

In order to do the best possible work, you ought for practice to have an exact copy of the disappearing mechanism used at Bisley; and also (and this is very important), the range should orientate as at Bisley and should have the background of the same colour.

At Bisley, at one time in the afternoon the shooting is against the setting sun; at which time the wise shot takes a rest and lets others waste their entries, as it is impossible to make good shooting under these circumstances. By having the points of the compass the same as at Bisley, you will soon find out which sort of light suits you best, and at what hour of the day it comes. Personally, I find the light from 9 to about 11 A.M. (during which time it is more or less over one's left shoulder) the best for shooting in July. As the sun comes round, you will find that the point to aim at varies gradually as the light strikes the front sight more or less on the side.

Variations in elevation, owing to varying intensities of sunlight, can also be remedied by having several pairs of spectacles with plain glass (unless, of course, you need optical glasses to see clearly with), of different tints of smoke or yellow colour. You can then, when you find a certain strength of light best for your shooting, keep to this strength artificially, whatever the real light may be, putting on glasses of a shade sufficient to modify the light as required. The glasses should have round, and not oval, frames, and these should be a good two inches in diameter, so that the rims do not interfere with your view. Large round goggles, with plain window-glass, are a great protection against particles of burnt-powder, especially in a head wind; and after a hard morning's shooting, the surface of the glass will be found covered with adhesive black spots. It is as well to have one pair of plain white glass (*i. e.*, ordinary window-glass), and to wear either these or one of the smoked or yellow pairs whenever shooting, or even looking on at shooting, as the powder blowing back constantly into the eyes irritates them; and a sudden dab in the eye may even spoil a score by making one flinch at a critical moment. I have known a man incapacitated from shooting for several days through getting his eyes inflamed from particles of powder and smoke blowing in his face in a head wind, and from the irritating fumes of the nitro-powders; and the look of many competitors' eyes towards the end of the shooting shows how it affects them. A solution of boracic acid and rose-water (of course you must get a chemist to dispense the right quantities) is a very good thing to bathe the eyes with during and after a hard day's shooting, and it makes the eyes feel very comfortable the next day.

Also, it is important to protect the ear-drums from the constant banging, else you get your ears "singing" and finally become more or less deaf. A pistol is worse than a rifle or gun in this respect, owing to the shortness of the barrel and the consequent proximity of the concussion to the ear. The left ear is more apt to suffer than the right, which is more sheltered by the arm, and a neighbour's shot, for which the ear is unprepared, affects it more than one's own. This is particularly noticeable if your neighbour stands slightly behind you. Some use cotton-wool in the ears. I find it apt to mix with the natural wax in the ears, a small amount of the cotton-wool remaining behind each time the wool is removed; and, what is more, it does not sufficiently deaden the sound. For practising in private, a pair of small down pillows tied over the ears deaden the sound best, or a racing motorist's skull cap with ear shields but both are very hot in warm weather and cannot be worn in public. "Elliot's Perfect Ear Protectors" are the best I have yet found; these are made in the United States and sold in England by Gieve Mathews & Seagrove, The Hard, Portsmouth. The concussion of pistols, bad at all times, is of course aggravated by the use of the heavy military ammunition obligatory at Bisley.

If you cannot get a copy of the Bisley disappearing-target mechanism, the next best thing is to have the target hinge over and be brought up again by some mechanical means. If this is not practicable, a stationary target may be made to answer, as I shall presently show.

My reason for wanting the actual Bisley arrangement is because that comes up with a jerk (some of the men operating it are very jerky), and the target "wobbles" for a fraction of a second, both just as it gets upright and just before it disappears, and this is apt to disconcert any one not used to it.

Next, get a metronome, with bell attachment. Set it to beat half-seconds (be very particular to get the time absolutely correct), and set the bell to ring at every sixth beat. You have now intervals of three seconds marked with a "ring" at the end of each. Count the beats to yourself when the metronome is working: "One, two, three, four, five, six"; "one, two, three," etc.

Get your man to work the lever which actuates the target (the lever in every case being a yard or two behind you, so that there is no danger of shooting the man or of burning his eyes with the side flash from the chambers of the revolver). Let him, at the stroke of the bell, bring up the target sharply, so that it comes with a bang, and lower it at the next ring in the same way, and keep it down till the next ring, then jerk it up, and so on; jerking it as roughly as the mechanism will allow.

If you have to practise on a stationary target, pretend to yourself that it disappears at each alternate ring of the metronome. The firing-point *must* be like the Bisley one; it will not do to stand with the revolver hanging at your side; it must rest on a ledge the same height as at Bisley, or else your practice will be useless for Bisley, as quite a different way of working the muscles and resting them between shots is in use in the two styles of shooting, and it takes less time to "come up" from a ledge than when the arm is hanging by the side. Owing to the slope of the ground at Bisley, some of the ledges are higher than others; choose the one that suits you best, and have your practice ledge that height; and when shooting at Bisley, do so from the ledge you have previously chosen.

Stand squarely, well behind this ledge. You will only get disqualified if you get into the way of resting the lower part of your body against the ledge; or even if you stand close to it and your coat happens to hang in front; or if you happen to have a "corporation" some competitor may have you disqualified as resting against the ledge.

The position of the legs and body is as for the twenty-yards stationary target, except that the rod which works the target is best kept between the feet, and these have to be a little wider apart. (N.B. If you are a short man, it is better to stand to one side of the rod.)

Stretch your arm out its full length, and, holding the pistol with the sights uppermost, rest the lower side of the barrel lightly against the ledge. The part of the barrel adjacent to the chamber is the part to rest on the ledge, as it is less likely to slip. There is a notch between the barrel and lower part of the frame of the revolver, and when this is resting on the edge of the table, and the arm is straight, then you are standing at the right distance from the table.

If you have to stretch too much or to lean forward, move slightly closer until you are comfortable; if your arm is bent, move backward till it comes straight. (All this is done with an *empty* revolver.)

Now stand in this position, watching the target go up and down, and counting all the while, "one, two, three," etc., to yourself, till you get the rhythm of the thing. Keep your eyes all the time fixed on the bull's-eye *when it is vertical to you*; do not follow it down with your eyes, but keep a mental picture of it, while it is away, on the background. You will gradually be able to know exactly *where* it will be, and *when* it will be there, and you will then be able to aim at the imaginary spot; so that when the target appears the sights will not have to be shifted to the bull's-eye, but *the bull's-eye will come to the sights*.

Now, cock the pistol, of course using only your right thumb, and not shifting your left hand, body, or pistol in the slightest.

(If you cannot do this neatly, cock the pistol first, and then "set" yourself at the ledge.)

Now, at the word "one," slowly (*i. e.*, without hurry or jerk) bring your arm up, quite straight, till the revolver is level with your eye, and you are looking through the sights.

If you have been following the above directions carefully, you will find you are aiming at the bottom edge of the bull's-eye, without having had to shift your hand or to align the sights; the sights and also the target have, in fact, "come up" to your eye, not your eye to them. The speed with which you raise your arm should bring the sights touching the bottom edge of the "bull" at the word "two"; but it is better, at first, to be slower: as long as you get the sights touching the "bull" before it disappears, it will do—for the present. At the word "six," lower the pistol to the table, but keep your eyes on the imaginary spot at which the "bull" disappeared. Keep the pistol down while you count six, and then raise it as before. After a few minutes of this drill, begin to squeeze the trigger slightly while the pistol is resting against the ledge. With practice you will be able to regulate the squeeze so that it will require only half a pound more pressure to fire the pistol. Then as you lift the pistol, gradually tighten the squeeze, and keep gradually tightening it, never diminishing the pressure, but not increasing it if your aim is getting wrong, and beginning to increase it again as you correct your aim. If you are increasing the squeeze properly, you will find, just as your aim is perfect, and a fraction of time before the word "six," the hammer will have fallen and you will not have jerked or moved off your aim. With an automatic pistol there is no need to cock it after the first shot, but with a revolver the instant the hammer has fallen, cock quietly with your right thumb, and lower your pistol to the table as before. In all cocking, I mean it to be understood that it must be done with one movement of the right thumb, the finger well clear of the trigger so as not to break or wear the sear-notch, and the left arm, left hand, and body not moved in any way, as already illustrated. After you have done this a few times, and have confidence, you may load several chambers of the revolver, having exploded, or empty, cartridges in the other chambers, so as not to injure the nose of the hammer or the mainspring. The cartridges, loaded and unloaded, should be put in in irregular order, and the barrel spun round, so that you do not know when you have a loaded one to fire.

Now, go through the same drill as before; most likely, if the first cartridge is an empty one, you will be surprised to find you jerked it off instead of squeezing, owing to fear of the recoil; but if this is so, expecting your next shot to be also an empty cartridge, you will give a nice, smooth, gradual "let-off," with the result that you will get a "bull," or close to it. The following shot, in consequence of your being too eager, will almost certainly be a very wild one, most likely below the target. This is caused by jerking the trigger, which results in bobbing the muzzle down. It is curious that, contrary to the usual idea that in firing quickly with a pistol one is prone to "shoot over," the exact reverse is the case, and that snatching at the trigger generally gives a low left shot. I have my pistols for rapid-firing competitions sighted to shoot higher than the others, to counteract this.

After a little of this sort of practice, you can get to loading all the chambers of a revolver. Now the great thing is "time." Time and shoot like a machine. At Bisley one sees men fire one shot directly the target appears; the next too late—after the target has begun to go down; and whenever a shot goes wide, they dance about, stamp, or swear, and shift their position constantly, half raise the pistol and lower it again, and more antics follow in the same fashion. A man who shoots in this style may as well go home, for all the prizes he will win. I never trouble to look at his target; seeing his "form" tells me what his target must look like.

By your constant practice with the metronome, you ought to get the "time" so impressed on your mind that you could work the target at the proper intervals without any metronome to indicate the time. Your hand "comes up" simultaneously with the target; you fire *just* before it disappears (some of my highest possibles were made with the target just on the "wobble" of disappearing as I fired each shot); every instant must be utilized for the aim, and there must be no hurry or flurry. In fact, you become a "workman."

Do not get into the trick of "coming up" too soon before the target appears. There is nothing to be gained by it, and you might be disqualified. If a shot goes wrong or there is a misfire (you are allowed another shot for a misfire), keep on just as though nothing had happened; pay no attention to the number of shots you have fired in the score, or how many more you have to "go." I have often started to "come up" again for a shot, not knowing that my sixth had already "gone," so mechanical had my shooting become.

In practice, never fire if you feel you are "off" the "bull"; better "come down" with the target, without shooting, and fire the next time the target "comes up." In this way you will perhaps "come up" ten times for your six shots; but you will have good shots for those that you have fired, and will be encouraged much more and get better practice than by firing a lot of wild shots, which as you fired, you knew were badly aimed.

At Bisley, I find this the easiest competition of any, more so, *if there is no wind*, than the stationary twenty-yards target, but one can only keep it up for a short time. One gradually gets into the swing of it, till one can "throw" each shot right into the "bull's" centre. This keeps up for a few entries; as one's arm tires, one begins to lose the absolute precision. It is then useless to continue shooting and it is time to take a rest.

You need a large front sight and open "U," so as to get your aim quickly. My favourite revolver has very coarse sights,—a front sight which, in aiming, seems nearly as large as the "bull."

I like the sun as much behind me as possible for this and any other quick-firing or moving-object competition, as you can then at once see the hit on the target and can correct it, if necessary, at the next shot. At a stationary target, this seeing the hit at once does not matter, as you have plenty of time to locate your shot with your telescope.

In any competition in which unlimited entries are allowed, it is best to give up shooting an entry at your first bad shot and to start a fresh entry instead of shooting out the full six shots. Many men say, "It is better to keep on, as it is practice." In my experience I find that everyone has strings of better shots than his average and these may commence at any time. If you have a three, for instance, as your second shot of a score, you may have four sevens to finish up with; then your next score may begin with two sevens and then a two. There are thus two scores spoilt, whereas, if you had retired at the shot counting three in your first score, and started another score, you would have had a string of six sevens in your second score, making a highest possible score of forty-two. I have so often seen this sort of thing happen to others (though I have never allowed it to happen to myself) that I am sure it is false economy at Bisley, except in the limited-entry series, not to stop and begin afresh the moment you get a shot out of the bull.

Another thing men do is to keep shooting pool to "get practice," as they call it, till they shoot themselves out and make bad scores in competition. The place to practise is *at home*; there is no economy in paying half-a-crown for every six shots at Bisley, when you can shoot as much as you like at home for nothing. The rapid-firing and fifty-yards competitions being more difficult, you may allow yourself one or two sixes in a score before beginning again; but stop at the first shot scoring less than six points.

If possible, choose a time when there is no one shooting at the target next you; as, even if you do not find yourself "letting loose" at the sound of his firing,—he most likely, timing himself all wrong,—the smoke from his shots may drift across you, and spoil your view of the target.

Do not shoot whilst a man is "arranging his things," or "bringing up his target" next you; it will distract your attention.

Shoot one entry in each series of competitions,—disappearing, rapid-firing, etc.,—and then take the competition in which you have done worst (comparatively worst, should be said, as thirty-six in the rapid-firing is equal to forty-one at the stationary twenty-yards) and beat that score. The moment you have beaten that sufficiently for one of your scores in another series to be the worst, go at that one; and so keep pushing the worst along. This gives you a better aggregate than any other system, and prizes are given for aggregates.

Be sure to look through your barrel after each entry, and wipe it out frequently. Quick shooting, especially in hot, dry weather, cakes and leads the barrel and spoils accuracy. If the pistol sticks or grates, however slightly, it is apt to spoil one's "time." At Bisley, you must not "wipe out" during the shots of an entry. Where, however, there is no rule against it, "wipe out" after every shot at stationary targets, and use only one of the chambers if using a revolver. When you open the revolver after each entry, look carefully to see if the caps were struck in the centre, especially if you have made a bad shot. Should they be hit on the side, clean the revolver; if this still continues, take another. It is useless to keep on while this is happening.

Be very careful to see that you are using your own ammunition, the proper sort for each particular pistol, and not taking some other that happens to be lying about. Also be very particular to have your pistol passed, the trigger-pull tested, and ammunition examined before shooting, by the official appointed for the purpose by the National Rifle Association, whose office is at the firing-point. This should be done every day, morning and afternoon,—as the trigger-pull may have altered,—so that there shall be no chance of disqualification after a good score is made.

Although it is, as a rule, best to finish your shooting at one class of competition, either moving or stationary, the change from one to the other gives a rest if you find yourself getting tired or discouraged. Moreover, as above explained, you secure a better "aggregate" by shifting from one series to another, though such changing would easily confuse a beginner. For the beginner, therefore, it may be as well to study one particular competition and compete in *it only* at Bisley the first year. This will probably place him high in the prize-list, and encourage further perseverance another year.

CHAPTER XI

STATIONARY FIFTY-YARDS TARGET

NOW we come to the fifty-yards target.

To shoot in this series (known as "The Long Range") you require the smallest and finest sights which you can see clearly without trying your eyes. There is no advantage in having them smaller than you can see properly.

Also, it is well to have several pistols with sights of different sizes, and differently sighted: some high, some low, some to the right, and some to the left, so as to suit varying light.

By the Bisley rules, you are not allowed to adjust your sights.

I have experimented with peep-sights; but one cannot hold a pistol steadily enough to get the full advantage of a peep-sight.

Have a Zeis glass and locate each shot, correcting the next, if necessary, by altering your aim—as the rules will not permit you to alter the sights; shoot very deliberately; rest your eyes frequently; stop at every breath of air, and only fire when you are "dead sure." Clean after each entry.

Do not keep on too long at this range. A few entries now and again are best, as it is very straining to the eyes and trying to the muscles.

I prefer a heavy charge, as giving more accuracy at fifty yards; but one cannot stand many shots with a heavy charge without feeling the consequences.

I do not think this deliberate shooting at fifty-yards at a stationary mark worth practising as a pistol is for quick shooting at a moving or momentarily appearing mark.

CHAPTER XII

TEAM SHOOTING AND COACHING

WHEN you are a member of a team, do exactly what the captain of the team directs you. Never mind if you think that he is wrong, and that you could do better work in your own way. It is "his show," and he alone is responsible; merely shoot as well as you can in his way. Of course, if he should ask your advice, that is a different thing. Should another member of your team ask your advice, refer him to your captain.

If you are captain of a team, and have the choice of men, select, preferably, men whose nerve can be relied upon; a veteran who does not get "rattled," even if only a moderate shot, is preferable to a brilliant beginner who may go all to pieces at a critical moment.

The man I prefer in a team is one who always shoots a good consistent score,—never brilliantly, yet never badly; you can always rely upon him to shoot up to his form. If you have two such men, let one of them shoot the first score,—if possible against your adversaries' best man,—so as to give your team confidence that they are likely to hold their own.

Reserve yourself—or your most reliable shot, who can be trusted not to lose his head—for emergencies, such as these: to shoot last, when everything depends upon making a good score; when the light is bad and likely to improve later; if there is a wind that may drop later; for pulling up a score when the other team is leading; for getting the sighting when you retire to the fifty-yards range; to shoot, "turn and turn about," against the most nervous or dangerous man of the other team, etc.

You should specially notice if any of your team are getting nervous; prevent their watching good shooting by their adversaries, or looking at and comparing scores. Encourage them to think that their own team is so strong that their own individual shortcomings do not matter. You can, in this way, "nurse" a man along who is on the verge of "going to pieces."

If possible, do not let your men know how the scores stand. If there is a wind, rain, or bad light, consult with your most "weather-wise" man, and decide how to "place" your bad shots so as to give them the easiest "shoot." That is to say, if the wind is likely to drop later, shoot your strong shots when the weather is unfavourable.

It is also a good thing to have a reliable member of the team stand behind each one who is shooting, to "spot" for him, keep time for him, and otherwise coach him, watching the time constantly, so as to let his man know *instantly*—if he asks—how much longer the time-limit allows him. Coaching is allowed in team shooting, *but not in ordinary individual competitions.*

Do not let any member of your team leave the range on any account till the competition is over.

Have a man or two extra, in case of anything disabling or preventing one of your team from shooting.

Do not let two men shoot with the same revolver, as both men may be wanted to shoot at the same time.

Do not scold a man, however badly he may be doing; you only flurry him, and it does no good.

Do not have any refreshments for your team until the competition is over.

CHAPTER XIII

SHOOTING IN COMPETITIONS

WHEN shooting in competition, be careful not to spoil your opponent's scores. Never approach or leave the firing-point while he is aiming or about to shoot. If he is about to shoot, and there be time, reserve your shot till he has fired; and do not fidget with your revolver or cartridges or get your target drawn up whilst he is aiming. Keep perfectly still and silent till his shot has gone off. Do not speak to him at any time, except to answer some question of his. If he is at all nervous, you might by a slight movement or word ruin his score.

Read carefully, *before* shooting, the rules of the competition in which you are about to engage, and be sure you comply with every detail of them. If you find you have, inadvertently, transgressed a rule, report to the range officer at once, and get your score cancelled.

Write your name very distinctly on your score-card; I have known a man to lose a prize owing to his name being illegible on the score-card. See that your shots have been entered properly and rightly added up and corrections initialled.

Have your target dated and signed by the range officer, with the name of the competition also inscribed, and keep it as evidence in case your card should get lost. Be sure you do not by mistake have a score entered on a ticket belonging to another series.

Before shooting in competition I put a weight in a chemist's scale equal to the *average* weight of one of my loaded cartridges. I weigh each cartridge against it; put all of the correct weight aside for Bisley, and keep the others for practice. By this means I minimize the chance of a weak or too strong shot.

When you are at the firing-point, pay no attention to what any one else is doing, or to what scores have been, or are being, made, or to any of your scores being beaten; the great thing is to have the average all round high for the aggregate prizes. If you are constantly watching the scores of others, rushing from range to range as your various scores are passed, you will have much less chance of making good scores than if you keep plodding on, constantly adding a point or two to your aggregate. You can afterwards try to beat individual scores, if necessary. Of course, if you at any time, in any one series, get a score which you think is up to the limit of your skill, you may let that series alone till you have reached your limit in another series.

Never watch a good man shooting; it will only make you doubt if you can beat him. It is also tiring your eyes uselessly.

Do not read or use your eyes any more than is absolutely necessary. When resting, dark glasses will be found a great relief to the eyes. I find that if I am getting tired of shooting, a half-hour's gallop on a horse that does not pull freshens me up, and helps to divert my thoughts; others may prefer lying quietly down and shutting the eyes.

If you find yourself getting stale, drop the whole thing, even for several days. It will not be time wasted, as you will shoot better afterwards; and you will certainly get worse if you keep on without rest.

Never protest or dispute a score or decision. The range officers are doing their best under very trying circumstances. If you think any decision wrong, say nothing about it and forget it; you will only spoil your shooting if you worry about it. Just set your teeth and make a score a point better than the disputed one ought, in your opinion, to have been. The protesting man is a nuisance both to himself and everyone else.

Should you see a man infringing the rules, leave it to others to protest.

CHAPTER XIV

DUELLING

THE mere word duelling appears to shallow minds a subject for so-called "humour," like mothers-in-law and cats, but a moment's thought will show that, in certain circumstances, the duel forms the only possible solution to a difficulty. And it is not an unmixed blessing that duelling is abolished in England as "Vanoc" in *The Referee* truly says. "For some reasons," he writes, "the abolition of duelling [he means in England] is a mistake. Insolent and offensive language is now too frequently indulged in with impunity.... The best rule of all is never to take liberties yourself, and never to allow liberties to be taken with you, and to remember that self-defence is still the noble art."

I think, though, that the still nobler art is the defence of others, and there are cases—which need not be gone into here—when a man *must* fight.

One of the reasons for this "humorous" attitude in the English mind (it does not exist abroad) is because sometimes abroad young men, wishing to advertise themselves, or their political ideas, fight duels, all the time never intending to hit each other, and in fact intentionally firing in the air.

When two good shots "mean business," a pistol duel is a very deadly affair, as is shown by the number of men who have been killed in them.

A duel with swords gives more advantage to a younger or a taller man, or to a man in the pink of condition, but a pistol duel will enable a much older man to hold his own.

The challenged has the right to choose weapons, and if he choose pistols it is understood that the meeting should be conducted with single-shot duelling pistols.

The British public are accustomed to confuse the words "pistol" and "revolver," and most pistol duels are described as "duels with revolvers" by those not understanding such things; but the revolver is not recognized as a duelling weapon, and any fight with revolvers would on the Continent lead to a trial for murder if any one were killed.

In challenging, the person considering himself aggrieved asks two of his friends to act as his seconds, and these he sends to his adversary. The latter at once appoints two seconds for himself, and the four seconds then make all the necessary arrangements.

First they call upon a gunmaker— combatants in a duel are not allowed to use their own weapons—and two single-shot muzzle-loading duelling pistols of regulation pattern are chosen.

In the presence of the seconds these are loaded by the gunmaker and put into a case, which is then sealed.

This case is taken to the duelling ground by the gunmaker and the seal is not broken until everything else is ready, the reason of course being to prevent tampering with the pistols, or loads, or obtaining practice with that particular pair of pistols.

A doctor is present at the duel with all necessary appliances.

On the ground the seconds draw lots for where their men are to stand, it being of advantage to have sun and wind at one's back, or left rear.

The distance is twenty-five metres, marked by canes stuck in the ground, and the shooters stand facing each other.

When all is in readiness, the seconds break the seal of the pistol case, then the director of the duel takes the weapons out, holding them by the barrels, one pistol in each hand, and presents the butt ends to the duellist to whom the lot has fallen to have first choice. The other pistol is handed to his adversary.

If shots are exchanged without result, the duellists exchange places for the next shot.

It is not permissible to try the trigger-pull by cocking and lowering the hammer, but about how light or heavy the pull is can be ascertained to some extent when cocking. A light click indicates a light pull, and a loud click a heavier one.

It is usual, especially if the duellists are good shots, and if they happen to be very angry with each other, to give them a very heavy trigger-pull in order to make it more difficult for them to hit each other. For the same reason the words of command in such cases are given very quickly. This prevents getting aim. It is well always to give a good strong pull back when firing, so as to avoid pulling off to the side if you have been given a very heavy trigger-pull.

Finally the duellists cock their pistols, the seconds stand clear, and the director of the fight stands midway between the duellists and about six metres back of the line between them.

The duellists stand with their right elbows touching their right hips, butt of pistol to thigh, and their pistols pointing at the ground.

The director calls: "Attention—Feu! Un—deux—trois!"

If either is not ready at the word "attention," he says so, but otherwise *after* the word "feu" he raises his pistol and must fire before the word "trois" is spoken.

If he does not have the butt of his pistol to his thigh, and muzzle to ground; or if he raises his pistol or even moves it before the word "feu"; or if he fires after the word "trois" has been spoken, and he kills his man, he is liable, if his adversary's seconds lodge a complaint, to be tried for murder.

The usual speed at which these words are spoken is a hundred words to the minute, but, as I have said, the director often hurries the words in order to baffle the duellists and prevent their injuring each other fatally.

Whether the duel should continue if neither combatant is sufficiently injured after the interchange of shots to prevent his going on shooting is a matter that the seconds have arranged between them before the duel begins. It depends chiefly upon the gravity of the reason for which the duel is fought.

The position to stand in, in my opinion, should not be quite sideways.

Of course one should, theoretically, make as small a target as possible for one's opponent, and therefore the coat should be buttoned close. But whereas if standing quite sideways one makes a smaller mark, if hit when in that position the wound will probably prove more dangerous.

A bullet which would perforate both lungs of a man standing sideways, will most likely go through one lung only if he be standing more full face. Several other internal organs are also safer when the shooters stand full face; by leaning forward the ribs are closer together and afford protection to the heart and lungs; also from a shooting point of view, one can make much better practice when standing more or less facing the object to be hit, than when craning one's head round to try and look over one's right shoulder, and so hampering one's right arm and straining the eyes.

It is generally considered that one should look as dark as possible to one's opponent, and turn up one's collar to avoid showing a white mark. But with this I am not sure that I quite agree. Personally I should prefer to shoot at an entirely black target without a white collar or white patch anywhere diverting one's eye, unless that white was at a place one wanted to hit.

But, if a very bad shot were going to fire at me, I should prefer his trying to hit my collar, as he would then be more likely to shoot over my head, or to miss me by shooting past me, than if he tried to hit me in the middle of the body.

The white collar would, however, be hidden by the right hand and pistol as soon as the pistol was raised, if aim were taken at an opponent's head.

The position safest *for yourself* is to aim at your opponent's head, and to get on to that position immediately after the word "feu," keeping your own head low.

Your right hand and the pistol-butt protect your throat and a good deal of your face and head if you lower your face as much as possible.

Some men stand in the position of lunging in fencing, which makes a still smaller target of the body, but then this exposes them to a more raking fire, and a shot which would only pierce the thigh of the right leg, if the duellist were standing upright, might glance along the thigh and penetrate the abdomen if he were standing in a lunging attitude, but it looks more manly to stand perfectly erect.

A level-headed man would never agree to fight a duel unless he deemed it justifiable, and then most likely his whole attention would be concentrated upon killing his opponent, and considerations of personal safety would be neglected; in the same way that a steeplechase rider thinks only of winning and not of his personal safety—if it is otherwise he is no good as a cross-country rider.

As the great object is to hit an opponent before he hits you,—as, if he hits you first, even slightly, he may spoil your aim,—it is better to hit him as low as possible, provided the bullet strikes high enough to injure him.

It takes time to raise the pistol to the level of his head, or even of his armpit, whereas with practice you can flip the wrist up and hit him in the thigh or hip without raising the arm at all, and immediately after the word "Un."

If you hit him in the thigh it would not be of much use in a serious duel, so the hip level is the point to try for.

An instance of perfect timing was that of a recent fatal duel where one man killed the other immediately after "feu," before his adversary had time to raise his pistol.

In the report of a certain duel which took place in France recently several of the English papers made stupid jokes because one of the duellists did not fire his pistol (he placed it behind his back) at the word "feu." The writers seemed to think he had forgotten to fire, because, when questioned as to why he did not fire, he answered, "*J'ai oublié*." Of course any one conversant with duelling would have known that by acting thus he meant that he did not desire to kill or to wound his adversary. A good shot who for any reason did not wish to hit his adversary would always put his pistol behind him rather than shoot wide and get credit for making a miss. It is more dignified to do this, if one does not want to shoot an adversary, than to miss on purpose. Moreover, the latter act might be misconstrued into an attempt to kill.

By French law, if a man is killed in a duel, the body must be left where it fell and the police informed at once. The police then make an investigation. The adversary is arrested and tried subsequently at the Court of Assizes. He ought, of course, to stop by the body and give himself up. He and his seconds may be condemned to imprisonment.

Not wanting to kill an adversary is also the reason so many duels are bloodless. Men, in the heat of an argument, challenge each other. In cooler moments, they see that the cause of quarrel was not of sufficient importance to warrant their killing, or attempting to kill, each other. Yet neither likes to apologize lest this should look like cowardice; so the two exchange a shot, and both miss on purpose.

In this connection I may mention that the American law does not apply in the case of a duel fought by a citizen of the United States outside the geographical limits of that country; for, according to Mr. R. Newton Crane, no offence is committed by the fact that an American citizen has participated in a duel beyond the jurisdiction of the United States. The citizenship of the combatant is, in such circumstances, immaterial.

"On the other hand," he continues, "sending, knowingly bearing, or accepting a challenge, in England or America, renders the sender, bearer, or accepter liable to punishment by the laws of England or America as the case may be, whether the duel is subsequently fought or not, and whether it is fought in England or America or abroad, and whether the offending party is an Englishman, American, or a foreigner. Provoking a man to send a challenge is also an indictable offence.

"The law applicable to the punishment for actually fighting the duel is, on the other hand, the law of the place where the duel is fought, and that law only applies to the offence.

"Provocation, however great, is no excuse, though it might weigh with the Court in fixing the punishment. Under the English law the punishment for sending, bearing, or accepting a challenge is fine or imprisonment without hard labour, or both. Each of the States of the United States has penalties for the offence, which though differing in detail are practically the same in substance as those provided by the English law."

Whilst for a revolver I advocate holding the thumb along the top of the grip, the stock is too straight for this hold with the duelling pistol, and the thumb must therefore be turned down.

How far you hold up the stock must be determined by practice. If you hold very high up, and you have a muscular or fat hand, the flesh between your thumb and forefinger will hide your hind sight. Hold it as high up as possible, however, and do not get too much of the forefinger round the trigger; also remember to squeeze straight back in practising for duelling.

A metronome to beat 100 to the minute is used. You cock the pistol and stand with the left foot behind the line of fire,—the right foot may be outside,—your elbow touching your hip, the butt of the pistol touching your thigh, and the pistol pointing at the ground.

Be very careful not to touch the trigger, as the pull is so light; be careful also not to point the muzzle at your right foot, for in that case you might put a bullet through your foot in the event of an accidental discharge.

The assistant, speaking at the speed of the metronome, says: "Attention! Feu! Un—deux—trois!" At the word "feu" you raise the pistol, which must be fired before the word "trois."

The target consists of a black figure of a man in profile. Shoot as I recommend at a disappearing target, but there are some differences.

Besides the grip and balance of the duelling pistol being different from those of the revolver, the pistol has to be raised from pointing to the ground, instead of from the hip level. This has a tendency to make you shoot low, as the time taken in raising the arm has to be hurried.

If your last shot was low, aim higher; if it was high, aim lower.

If you are careful to squeeze, instead of jerking, you are almost sure always to hit the figure, the only misses allowable being a graze of the waist to the left, or under the chin to the right.

Doctor Devilliers has patented a bullet for practising duelling, the competitors shooting at each other. The bullet is useful also for indoor shooting where a leaden bullet would be dangerous.

The composition of the bullet is a secret, but the bullet is light, and, when propelled by a cap with fulminate only, gives a hard rap where it strikes.

When shooting with it at a man the following precautions must be observed, according to the inventor.

1. "Don't shoot at less than twenty metres." It is useless to shoot with it at more than twenty metres, as the bullet rapidly loses its accuracy beyond that distance; the blow at twenty metres distance is not severe if one is properly protected against it.

2. "Wear goggles, a fencing mask, and gloves." The goggles are now made part of the mask, and are of very thick glass, while instead of the shooter's wearing a glove, a metal shield is affixed to the pistol. *The hand must not be lowered before your opponent fires.* I once shot against a friend who omitted this precaution, and my bullet cut away the flesh at the lower part of his thumb.

3. "Wear a black linen blouse." This may be necessary to prevent your clothes being soiled, but it makes you a bigger target for your opponent. Therefore a tight-fitting coat is better. I shoot with no body protection.

4. "In winter be careful that the bullets do not freeze." I find it best to keep the loaded pistols on ice for some time before shooting—not letting them freeze, however—and not to let the pistol get too hot, for if the barrel gets hot the bullet does not take the rifling.

CHAPTER XV

SHOOTING OFF HORSEBACK

WHEN shooting off a standing horse at a stationary mark, turn the horse facing to the left at an angle of forty-five degrees. This is to prevent his flinching at the shots, as any but a very seasoned horse would be sure to do if you shot straight over his head or close past his ears. Also, if he were to toss his head when you were shooting over it, you might both kill him and get either a rearing backward fall, with the horse on top of you, or else a "purler" over his head. If the horse shies away from the outstretched arm, tie a handkerchief over his off eye, as the bullfighters do, until he is accustomed to the noise and flash.

There should be a bar in front of the horse to prevent his getting closer to the target than the distance for which the match is arranged; but if the bar is low, and the horse a good fencer, he is apt to jump at the bar. It is very difficult to get a horse to keep absolutely still, and for that reason it is often more difficult to shoot when the horse is fidgeting than when he is swinging along in a gallop.

For shooting on a gallop or canter, the French rubber balloons filled with water, put up on the "heads and posts" principle, are very good marks, as they can be shot at with wooden or Devilliers bullets, shooting alternately to the right and left. These rubber balloons are filled with water by a syringe which can be set to inflate them to any size, and the mouth of the balloon is closed by simply squeezing the metal mouth together. I can also recommend a target on the principle of the Bisley "running deer," travelling on rails parallel to a railing, on the other side of which the shooter gallops and which prevents his getting too close to the target.

Firing blank ammunition at "lightning paper" stuck in the cleft of a stick is very good practice. The paper flares up on being touched by burning particles of powder, but of course the shooting must be done at a distance of a few feet only.

I do not think there is much advantage in cantering too slowly; the speed at which the horse goes smoothest, without raking or boring, is the best.

For practical purposes, shooting behind one, when galloping, is useful. This is, I think, best practised with blank ammunition at the lightning paper, or with Devilliers bullets, otherwise it would be too dangerous. It is an assistance, when first learning, to catch hold of the pommel of the saddle with the bridle hand as you swing your body round to fire. When shooting alternately to right and left, be sure to lift the muzzle of the revolver clear of the horse's head as you swing it from side to side, or you may shoot your horse through the head, if he should happen to toss it at that moment.

It is useless to try to shoot off a horse unless both you and your horse understand "school" riding. An ordinary hunter, ridden in the ordinary hunting style, needing both hands to lug at his head, and requiring half a field to stop or turn him in, is very dangerous at this game.

The horse must turn, change legs, stop dead, and start again under the control of one hand only.

A horse that naturally leads with his near leg when allowed to choose his own lead is preferable, as, having to range up on the near side of the mark, you can shoot better leading on the near leg, as this turns you slightly towards the mark. A horse is smoothest in his natural lead, and is rougher and consequently more difficult to shoot off when leading on the other leg.

One can wear the holster as the cowboys do—a belt round the waist and the revolver hanging on the right hip, not round the waist in front as army men carry it. In front it is in the way of your bridle hand, and it is not so handy to draw; but, worn on the hip, it is also dangerous in case of a fall, and is perhaps best in a saddle holster.

The revolver must fit loosely, so as to draw easily; but the holster must be deep enough, and must hang so as not to drop the pistol out in galloping. The flap of the saddle—where the hunting-horn is carried—is a good place to hang the holster, but this arrangement might hurt one if the horse rolled over; and one might be left defenceless by the horse galloping off with the pistol.

I prefer a short-cheeked, single-rein curb with a loose curb-chain.

Why do writers so often talk of "pressing with the *knee*" to turn a horse? One uses the *knees* to grip with and the *legs* for turning and collecting, etc.

I do not recommend a martingale if it can possibly be avoided, as it is apt to throw a horse down.

CHAPTER XVI

PISTOL SHOOTING FOR LADIES

A PISTOL puts the weakest woman, who is a good shot, on an equality with the strongest man. It is especially suitable for ladies to defend themselves with, as they have, as a rule, steadier hands than men, and there are certain pistols, just suited for ladies, which give no recoil, and yet are practical weapons. "U. M. C." gallery ammunition in a big .44 calibre Smith & Wesson Russian Model gives practically no recoil, and I have seen a lady do very good target shooting with it. With this revolver and load I have killed three rabid, or alleged rabid, dogs, so it is a practical killing load. I use the same revolver and ammunition for shooting park bucks.

Every lady should, to my mind, know how to use a pistol. She may at any time be in China or some other country where there are savage natives; and there is none of that danger of bruising the body which is so harmful to ladies using guns or rifles.

The Smith & Wesson hammerless safety revolvers of .38 and .32 calibre are especially suitable for self-defence for ladies; but I should not recommend a lady to use these or any other short, light self-defence revolvers unless it be actually necessary, as the recoil is heavy and apt to hurt a lady's hand (particularly between the first finger and thumb) and tear the skin. This is inevitable in a revolver made as light and as portable as possible, and expected, nevertheless, to shoot a very heavy charge.

The best plan is to fire a few shots (the hand being protected with a thick driving glove, from which the forefinger has been cut off), or, better still, ask a good shot, who also knows your "sighting," to do so for you, just to get the sights filed right, and then keep this pistol for self-defence only, and do practising and competing with a more accurate and more pleasant shooting weapon.

The pistol to be used for practice and in competitions must depend upon your physique. If you are moderately strong, I think the .44 Russian Model Smith & Wesson, with the Union Metallic Cartridge Co.'s gallery ammunition, is as good as any; or, if this is too heavy, the .38 or .32 calibre Colt and Smith & Wesson revolvers, with gallery ammunition, are very good and are specially intended for the use of ladies. The first-named revolvers are no longer made, but the solid frame revolvers of the same make and calibre are very suitable also, if shot with a gallery charge, if a second-hand Russian model revolver cannot be found.

The Smith & Wesson .32 calibre in .44 calibre frame, which I like for fifty-yards target shooting is rather heavy for a lady. Ladies who are of slight build may find it too heavy; but with gallery ammunition it has no recoil whatever, which is a great advantage for ladies.

Always have a barrel not shorter than five inches and not longer than six inches, and save the weight, if you want a light weapon, in the general makeup of the revolver, fluted barrel, etc., not in length of barrel, as you lose so much accuracy with a three-inch or four-inch barrel that it spoils any pleasure in shooting.

If you confine yourself to light ammunition, you can get a very light revolver which is safe with *that* charge, and has no recoil to speak of.

The Smith & Wesson, which has interchangeable barrels of .32 calibre for revolver, and .22 for single-shot pistol, is a very suitable weapon for a lady.

The lighter forms of single-shot Stevens pistols of .22 calibre are exceptionally well adapted to the use of ladies who prefer a single-shot pistol. The Colt .22 calibre revolver is very nice for ladies' use.

In mentioning particular firms, both here and elsewhere in this book, I must not be understood to mean that the weapons of any one maker are better than those of another. All first-class makers turn out good revolvers and pistols; and I merely mention those revolvers and pistols which I have used and am personally acquainted with, and which I find answer my requirements.

A lady can carry a pistol hidden for self-defence in many more ways than a man, owing to her draperies affording more places for concealment. Cloaks, capes, etc., make good hiding-places for a pistol; inside a muff is about one of the best places; and a small pistol in the right hand, inside a muff, that hand hanging down by the side, is ready for instant use. As ladies often carry their muffs in this way, it does not arouse suspicion.

It is very important for ladies to protect their ears when shooting, with Elliot ear protectors.

CHAPTER XVII

STAGE SHOOTING

THIS subject can be subdivided into two parts: real, expert, very accurate work, requiring great skill and nerve; and conjuring tricks, that is to say, shooting assisted by apparatus and the arts of the conjurer. The greatest insult that can be offered to a professional shot is to call him a conjurer.

To begin with the unaided shooting: You must have a safe background to shoot against. The best, in my opinion, is a steel plate, leaning towards you at an angle of forty-five degrees, and below it a shallow tray, filled with sand, to catch the bullets, which flatten on the steel and drop into the tray. As only very light powder-charges are used, and as the bullets for this purpose are round, or semi-round, this is sufficient.

It is usual to have something for the bullets to go through before striking the steel plate. Green baize is good for the eyes as a background; but it is dangerous, being very inflammable; it gives off fluff, some of which stands out from the baize, and the rest falls to the ground. This is like tinder and is liable to catch fire from burning particles of powder. Some fabric dipped in a non-inflammable mixture should be used; either green, white, or black, whichever you find suits your eyesight best. The butt is either put "prompt" side of the stage (so that the shooter's right arm is nearest the audience), and at a slight angle, in order that people may see the target; or it is placed at the back of the stage, the shooter standing with his back to the audience. In either case, the shooter keeps his "tools" on a side-table, and when he shoots he stands quite clear of any table, so as to afford an uninterrupted view of all his proceedings.

The range is about fifteen feet. This may seem very short, but it looks a long shot on a stage; and it must be remembered that the shooting is at very small objects and no misses are allowable. The golden rule to be borne in mind in stage shooting is: Never hazard a shot that is not very easy to you, and which you cannot be practically sure of successfully accomplishing. If you try a difficult shot and succeed once in three times—such as hitting a cork thrown into the air—hardly any of the audience will think of you as aught but a bad shot; whereas, if you hit six stationary glass balls—each as big as an orange—in rapid succession, they will think you wonderful! Several professional self-styled champion pistol shots, use both hands to hold their pistols which is never allowed in any pistol competition, and stamps them as no pistol champion.

WEAPONS

One or more .44 Russian Model Smith & Wesson target revolvers; Ira Paine target sights; hair-trigger; Union Metallic Cartridge Co.'s gallery ammunition. I use the revolvers which formerly belonged to Ira Paine; several front sights, the finest about the size of the head of a small pin, the stalks as fine as a needle; hind sight adjustable, both laterally and vertically, with screw adjustment; trigger-pull so light that laying the finger on the trigger almost sets it off. With such a revolver, of course, extreme care must be taken never, for an instant, to have the barrel pointed in any direction except that in which it would be safe for the bullet to travel, and also to keep the finger off the trigger till you actually want the bullet to go.

Ira Paine when shooting at objects on the head of an assistant, used to "come down" from above, instead of "coming up" in the usual way; so that if the pistol went off by accident there would be no danger to the assistant, as there would be if the muzzle travelled up his body to his head in sighting from below.

I do not approve of shooting at objects on the head or in the hands of an assistant; it is not, in my opinion, justifiable to risk life in this way.

The other weapon is a Stevens, or Smith & Wesson, single-shot .22 pistol. Some people use this to give variety to the show; but I prefer a duelling pistol.

See that a narrow plank of wood—metal would, if struck, make a bullet glance—is put in front of the butt with slits and clips in it for holding objects. As mentioned before, I do not like assistants holding them in the fingers, though, for this purpose, steel thimbles are generally worn over the thumb and forefinger, and are concealed by a glove.

Professionals sometimes shoot objects on the heads of assistants—generally a lady with her hair piled up very high, or wearing a steel skull-cap under a wig. Devilliers bullets make such shooting practically safe in case of the assistant being hit.

The following shots I recommend to amateurs as safe. Beginning with the easiest, we have:

Six stationary balls in a row or else the French rubber balloons. (The balls are cast from a mixture of resin and whiting; they are very brittle and break at a graze.) Take them as quickly as you can be sure of them. With practice, you can "snap" the six off in about four seconds.

Next extract the used cartridges, and have them put in a row on the edge of the board, standing them on their bases. Hit them in quick succession.

This requires a little more care, as they are small; but their height prevents your being likely to miss vertically, and you have merely to pay attention to keeping your horizontal aim correct. Be sure not to shoot too low; for if you do, and hit the plank, you will jar all of them off it.

This can be varied, if you are a really good shot, by placing the spent cartridges on their sides with the cap end towards yourself; but it requires good shooting.

Shooting at an object with a wine glass on each side without breaking the glasses is a trick in which the difficulty varies according to how close the glasses are.

Put up a piece of paper with a black pencil line ruled vertically on it; hit this line. This requires care not to "pull off" to one side.

A similar line horizontal. This is more difficult, as the elevation must be absolutely correct if you want to hit the line.

Hit a swinging ball. Take the shot on a turn; do not follow, but aim at an imaginary spot just inside of where the ball is at one end of its swing, aiming at "IX o'clock," as the ball is momentarily stationary at its farthest swing to the right, or *vice versa*.

Put six balls in a row; hit one with the revolver in the right hand, a second with the revolver in the left; a third and fourth with the revolver upside down, pulling the trigger with the little finger and using alternate hands. The remaining two shots to be made with the revolver held half canted to the right, and then half canted to the left. After a little practice, none of these positions are difficult.

The upside-down shot, as soon as you get used to aiming at the top edge of the ball instead of the bottom, is a very steady, easy position. For the two side ones, you aim at "IX" and at "III o'clock," respectively.

Hang your watch on a hook on the board, and place a ball resting on this hook. Break the ball. This is easy, as the ball is, comparatively, a big mark. Aim at the top edge of the ball, so as to break it by a grazing shot near the top; this is less risky for the watch.

Do the same with any watches lent by the audience. A man once kept lending me his watch for this trick; I found out afterwards that it would not go, and he had hoped that I would hit it and thus be compelled to give him another!

Borrow small objects from the audience, and hit them. Stamps on envelopes, visiting cards, bits of pencil, etc., are suitable; but do not shoot at anything which will make a bullet glance, or you may hit some of your audience. Thus a walnut is very dangerous, causing bullets to glance. An orange or an egg explodes beautifully when hit, but both are rather messy. The coloured balls for Christmas trees are nice to shoot at; but a bullet sometimes makes a hole without breaking them.

Put up the ace of hearts and hit it. It is usual to have a pack composed of only aces of hearts. Have several ace cards placed on top of each other, and when the bullet goes through the group, have the cards "dealt" among the audience; or, if at a Charity Bazaar, sold singly.

Put up the six of hearts, and hit the six pips. This requires some doing to get all six shots neatly in the separate pips.

Put a card edgeways towards you and cut it in half. This is a pretty trick and brings down the house when well done. It requires the same skill as hitting the vertical pencil lines. If you are not very sure of yourself, and you succeed on the first shot, do not risk a second try. *This rule applies to all the difficult shots.* My best score at this game was five cards out of six shots, the cards being placed edgewise at a range of fifteen feet.

Hit a string from which an object is hanging. Get string which is weak, and have the object pretty heavy, or else you may "nick" the string without its breaking. Berlin wool, with a weight so heavy that it strains the wool to nearly breaking-point, breaks with more certainty than string or twine. There is an ingenious, though scarcely legitimate, way of making this shot very easy. You merely double a piece of string and tie a knot, hanging it over two nails, the distance between which is a fraction under .44 inch. Two hooks on the ball are the same distance apart, so that the ball is thus hung by a double string. If you hit *between* these, *both* strings are necessarily cut by a .44 bullet, if your aim be true, while *one* is cut even if you hit half an inch out.

Put a rubber balloon filled with red fluid on top of an empty claret glass; break the ball, and the glass will be filled with the fluid. Take care the ball fits very loosely, and rests only slightly in the glass, or the latter will break also.

Knock a cork off a bottle; an ordinary wine bottle or a wooden or metal one is dangerous if hit, as causing the bullet to glance; it is better to have a plaster of Paris bottle, painted black.

Put up a bunch of six grapes, and take them off one at a time.

Put up candles and snuff them.

Hit two balls simultaneously, one swinging past a stationary one, or both swinging from opposite ways. You have to take them just as one is about to cover the other.

Have a ball swung round horizontally at great speed centrifugally from a small wheel spun by clockwork. This requires very good "timing," you aiming at a side and pulling when the ball is at the opposite side, or you will be too late. Stand two balls with a steel knife-edge between them, vertically towards you and rather nearer to you than the balls. Hit the knife-edge in such a manner as to split the bullet in two pieces, which fly off and break the balls. The knife must be securely fastened, and the precise distance between the back of it and the balls (which varies according to the distance they are apart) must be determined by experiment. Trick shooters use shot for this instead of a bullet.

Hitting an object with a paper on the muzzle hiding the mark. Cut a round hole, just big enough to slip over the muzzle, in a piece of thick paper the size of an ordinary envelope. Slip this over the muzzle, up against the front sight. When taking aim, it will be found that with the left eye closed the paper hides the object. By keeping both eyes open, however, shooting is easy, the right eye working the sights and the left seeing the object. The paper must not project much to the left, or it would hide your view with the left eye.

Fix a nail slightly in a block of soft wood and drive it home with a shot.

CHAPTER XVIII

TRICK SHOOTING

WE now come to the conjurer's style of shooting, which I would not advise any one to practise, even for a Charity Bazaar; it will ruin his reputation as a shot. However, I will describe hereunder some of the devices in connexion with this trick shooting.

The chief apparatus—under different forms—is a lever some twelve inches long. This lever is pivoted in its centre; one end has a steel disk about a foot in diameter, or less, according to the shooter's skill—of a size he is sure of never missing,—the other end has a steel point at right angles. The lever is placed vertically at such a height that the steel spike is just opposite the middle of the ball which is placed on the assistant's head. The steel disk is some eight inches above the man's head; the whole of this apparatus is hidden from the audience behind the "back-cloth" of the scenery. The locality of the disk is indicated to the shooter by something in the scenery, as a pattern, or a trophy of flags, etc.

The assistant stands with his back against the back-cloth, and the ball is on his head so that the steel spike is just clear of the middle of the ball; the shooter then fires at the trophy of flags, or what not (which is eight or more inches above the man's head, and therefore a practically easy and safe shot); the bullet hitting the disk, drives it back; the other end of the lever with the spike comes forward; the spike goes through the scenery, breaks the ball, and at once returns out of sight. The trick is varied by having the lever inside a dummy figure, the performer shooting into the figure to break small objects on its head or in its mouth. A bellows is sometimes behind the back-cloth with the nozzle at the flame of a candle which is blown out when the bellows is hit; and the shooter is supposed to have snuffed the candle.

The shooting can be done at quite long range from the back of the gallery to the back of the stage (for instance) by lengthening the lever so as to minimize risk to the assistant.

Another way in which the candle trick is done, is to have each candle inside a large concave reflector; the splash from the bullet comes back from the reflector and puts out the candle.

Shooting at anything moving—swinging balls, etc.—is done with shot; the shooting in this case must be done with a back-cloth over the butt, as the splashes on a naked steel plate would betray the use of shot. This makes very easy what in legitimate shooting requires nice "timing." The cartridge is either simply filled with special shot even smaller than "dust" shot and a wad, or if the cartridges are likely to be seen they are loaded with hollow wooden black-leaded bullets, full of shot, which the rifling of the barrel breaks, and these are substituted by "palming" for real bulleted cartridges shown to the audience. Shot is sometimes fired out of a smooth bore revolver.

Two balls are broken with a revolver in each hand, shot simultaneously. This is always considered very wonderful, the performer pretending to take a long time over his aim, etc. One revolver is loaded with shot, the other with blank ammunition. The one loaded with shot is aimed between the two balls; the spread of shot breaks both balls.

Knocking ashes off cigar whilst being smoked by assistant: A long hat-pin is put into the cigar, the point just reaching up to the ashes. On the shot—a blank cartridge—being fired, the assistant pushes the knob of the pin with his tongue, and dislodges the ashes.

Objects held in the fingers or resting on the shoulders of assistants are shot with cork or Devilliers bullets, and the assistant wears hidden steel epaulets and finger-tips.

Blindfold shooting is done by seeing down the side of the nose on to a looking-glass fixed at an angle behind the hind sight.

What is called shooting through a wedding-ring and breaking a ball is done with the lever apparatus; the bullet does not go through the ring, but above it.

Shooting at the trigger of a loaded rifle fixed in a rest, the shot from the rifle breaking a ball on the shooter's head, is also another form of the lever apparatus.

I think that in stage performances there should be a committee of shooting men appointed by the audience to see that the shooting is genuine and not trick shooting.

CHAPTER XIX

SHOOTING IN SELF-DEFENCE

THIS chapter is written entirely from the technical point of view as a branch of pistol shooting, while the legal aspect of the question is treated by law experts in the Appendix of my larger treatise, *The Art of Revolver Shooting*. Fortunately, however, in the great majority of cases, the object of protecting oneself—or, what is more important, protecting someone else—is attained without actually shooting. The mere fact of being armed is generally sufficient, and in many cases wearing the revolver openly or having it in one's hand, even unloaded, suffices. As Polonius says: "Beware of entrance to a quarrel, but being in, bear't that the opposed may beware of thee." But, if shooting *has* to be done, everything depends on *getting the first shot*.

I am *not* dealing with the ethical aspect of the case; and, putting *that* aside, if you can take your adversary unawares, and "get the drop on him" before he gets it on you, you have a great advantage.

A short-barrelled pistol is best if it has to be concealed, but of as big a calibre as you can carry without its being too bulky and showing in your pocket. If there is no necessity for concealment, carry one six inches in the barrel.

Some prefer a large-bore army revolver, with the barrel cut down to two inches. I am assuming that the shooting will be done at a distance of only a few feet, and without aim in the ordinary sense of the word.

It is very dangerous to carry an automatic pistol loaded in the pocket, unless it has a safety bolt.

The proper way to carry a revolver (unless a "safety revolver" is carried) is to leave one chamber unloaded, and lower the hammer on that empty chamber. The revolver here described obviates these risks.

This is the Smith & Wesson .38 calibre safety hammerless pocket revolver. This revolver cannot go off accidentally, even when all the chambers are loaded, as there is a safety catch which prevents the revolver being discharged unless it is pressed at the same time that the trigger is pulled.

Any one used to revolver shooting, who holds this revolver as I have described in my instructions for revolver shooting, and *squeezes the trigger*, will be able to shoot without thinking of the safety catch, for he presses it unconsciously in gripping the stock. A person not accustomed to a revolver cannot, however, fire it; in fact, if a man not an expert revolver-shot wrested the revolver from you, it would be harmless in his hands against you. Indeed, the pistol could without danger be given, loaded, to a small child to play with, as it requires a stronger grip than a child's to discharge it.

Most revolver accidents occur either from the hammer receiving an accidental blow, slipping from the thumb, catching in something, or from the trigger being touched unintentionally, or the revolver being left at full-cock.

In this Smith & Wesson safety revolver all these causes of accident are impossible, and it is always ready for instant use. Its further advantages are:

1. There is no external hammer to catch in anything.

2. Pressure on the trigger cannot discharge the revolver unless the stock is properly grasped at the same time.

3. The revolver cannot be kept at full-cock.

4. Being hammerless, and having no projections, it can be drawn more quickly than an ordinary revolver.

5. It can be carried with absolute safety loaded in the pocket, with the knowledge that a fall or blow will not discharge it.

This revolver is also made in smaller calibre (.32), with both 3 in. and 1½ in. barrel. In the latter case it is called a bicycle revolver, and takes up less room in the pocket.

This calibre might be better for a lady's use; but for a man I prefer the large calibre, as being more powerful.

The cocking by trigger action in this revolver is so arranged that it can, with a little practice, be held at full-cock whilst the aim is taken, instead of the cocking and firing being a continuous action, as in other double-action revolvers. As to its accuracy I can put all the shots in a "man" target at twenty-five yards with it.

Carrying the pistol in the hip pocket is in my opinion a mistake, as the movement of putting back the hand to draw will instantly put an adversary on his guard and most likely draw his fire.

For a case where you are likely to be robbed, the inside breast-pocket (where bank-notes are usually carried) is a good place for the pistol, as, when you are asked for your money, you can appear to be taking it out of this pocket whilst you are really drawing the pistol, or it can be shot from this pocket without drawing it.

Usually the right-hand side-pocket of a jacket is the handiest, or, rather, the pocket on the side of the hand you can shoot with best.

Shooting through the pocket is as quick and unexpected a way as any; another is to turn partly away, and in doing so draw and fire from behind your back, or under your other arm.

But, assuming that you would prefer, if possible, to capture your assailant without shooting him, try whether you cannot unexpectedly "get the drop" (*i. e.*, an aim) on him, and make him hold up his hands before he can draw his revolver.

As in fencing and boxing, the great thing is never to take your eyes off your opponent's for an instant; and if by any subterfuge you can induce him to take his eyes off you, or distract his attention to anything else, then is the time to "get the drop" on him, or, as a last resource, to shoot.

Knocking a chair over, throwing something past or at him, with your non-shooting hand, or calling out to some imaginary, or real, person behind him may often have the desired effect.

If he is a really "bad" man, and armed, the worst thing you can do is to take a pistol in your hand—or even make towards it—unless you mean to shoot instantly; it will only draw his fire, or he may unexpectedly disarm you in the way described below.

Supposing you are unarmed and your adversary has a pistol, you may be able to render his weapon harmless by ejecting his cartridges. This does not apply to an automatic pistol.

The way to do this varies with different makes of revolvers, but the principle in each case consists in making a downward stroke on the barrel of his revolver with one of your hands, and in the same movement operating the opening catch or lever with your thumb.

If you get an assistant to take an empty revolver and point it at you, and you practise this trick, you will find it very simple and effective, but of course there would be no use in trying it with an adversary who suspected you were about to do so. The Smith & Wesson Russian Model can be rendered harmless by seizing the middle of the barrel with your thumb under the catch, you being to the left and using your right hand, or *vice versa*. Simultaneously with seizing the revolver give a quick quarter turn to your wrist to the right, and all the cartridges will fly out.

With the Webley, you place your thumb OVER instead of *under*, the catch in seizing the revolver, and press your thumb towards the palm of your hand in making the wrench.

With solid frame revolvers, like the new Colt and Smith & Wesson, you operate the catch, and instead of twisting your wrist, you push out the cylinder with your first and second fingers, at the same time pushing the extractor plunger with your little finger, but this make of revolver is much more difficult to disarm suddenly than those I have named above.

With any hammer automatic pistol or revolver you can make it harmless by slipping your thumb under the hammer, or, in the case of a revolver, if you are strong in the grip, by holding the cylinder and preventing it revolving after the first shot is fired.

I saw a very good suggestion in an article in an American paper—the writer's name I unfortunately forget—to the effect that it was an excellent thing, when expecting "trouble," to wear a big revolver ostentatiously and to have a smaller one in your hand, concealed under a cape, or otherwise; your adversary would think himself safe as long as he watched your big revolver and saw that you had not put your hand near it, whilst all the time you would be ready to "hold him up" or shoot with the other pistol, the existence of which he would not suspect.

If a burglar is in your house, do not carry a candle, as that makes you an easy target in case he should try to shoot at you. The pistol which is sighted by projecting a light would simply give the enemy an easy aim. The iron rails of banisters, especially if they are wide, ornamental ones, are a good protection. A door is of no use (except for concealment *before* the man has seen you), as a bullet with an ordinary charge will go through it.

Use a light charge revolver (gallery ammunition by preference) for house protection; with an automatic pistol you may shoot some of your family through a thin wall when "burglar-potting."

Out-of-doors, too, a lamp-post, or other narrow object, will spoil a man's aim by making him try to hit that part of you which shows on either side instead of his having your full width to aim at, even if it is too narrow or small fully to protect you.

It is better not to try to give him a small mark to aim at by standing sideways, as then, if he hits you, he will rake all through your vitals; whereas, if you are facing him squarely, he may put several bullets into you without fatal effect. Holding your bent arm across your heart, and at the same time protecting your temples with the side of your pistol—which duellists do directly they have fired,—may be of some use; but it is better to depend upon hitting your adversary before he hits you. If he shoots and misses you, drop at once, as if hit, and he will probably pause and give you a chance to shoot.

If a man does not look desperate and capable of continuing shooting till he is killed, if you can break his shooting wrist it may be sufficient; and if he should try to shift his pistol from the disabled hand to the other, you can break that also.

Should you be mounted and your adversary afoot, jumping off and sheltering yourself behind your horse will protect you from a revolver-shot; but not an automatic pistol; also galloping hard at him and shouting may spoil his aim; but if he is cool he may take an easy shot at you when you are past and before you can turn.

If a man is running away from, or coming at you, and has no firearm, you can make him helpless by shooting him in a leg; a long crossing shot in a bad light would make the leg shot rather doubtful, unless there be time to have several tries.

If a man absolutely has to be killed, it is better to shoot where the white shirt shows in evening dress. This is a bigger mark than the head, and he may, moreover, duck his head as you pull.

The stomach shot is a murderous one, and would not be justifiable except under very rare circumstances. A charging man at very close range would have the wind knocked out of him, and be stopped perhaps more effectually by this shot than any other.

If your opponent is a bad shot, you can take a long shot at him from a distance, say 120 yards, at which, if he has a cheap revolver, he cannot hit you except by a fluke.

In fact, a bad shot armed with a pistol is less dangerous than a strong, determined man with a knife. It must be remembered that a knife can be thrown some distance, so it does not do to let a man with one in his hand, or even suspected of having one, come too close.

A cartridge loaded with salt is a good man-stopper for burglars and has the advantage of not endangering life, but of course it is of no use against a determined man unless he is shot in the face; and in that case salt might do even more damage to his eyes than a bullet, and a bullet would be a more merciful load.

The writer of a small pamphlet entitled *Self-Defence* says that to put the pistol beside the head of the bed, or under the pillow, is to court being disarmed during your sleep, and recommends having it between the mattresses, handy to your reach, or in a padded bag hanging at the side of your bed under the sheets, the object of the padding being to prevent the pistol making a noise against the bed when you are drawing it.

This is all very well if you remember to take out the pistol each morning; if you forget, and the housemaid makes up the bed roughly, there may be trouble.

It also advises rolling under a bed or sofa as a precaution when exchanging shots.

Make sure that nobody can tamper with your pistol or cartridges. I knew of a case in which a muzzle-loading revolver was kept loaded in an unlocked box at the side of the bed. When there was a burglary in the house, this revolver was found to have been *dipped in water* and thus rendered useless!

CHAPTER XX

SHOOTING IN THE DARK

THERE are occasions on which it is necessary to shoot at night, as for a night-watchman; or in the case of a wild animal's jumping into camp and carrying off someone; or in night attacks. For this work, an exceptionally large *dead white* front sight (either a fixed one or an adjustable one on a hinge) is needful. This sort of sight, though, can only be seen if there is moonlight, or at least some glimmer of light.

In pitch-darkness, a large front sight with both itself and the rib of the barrel coated with luminous paint is useful, provided the pistol is, for several hours previous to being used, exposed to strong sunlight. If it is kept all day in a case or holster, the paint will not shine at night. Also, in cleaning the pistol, the paint may be spoilt and may require renewing. I would not advise painting any pistol you care about.

The most satisfactory way is to learn to shoot in the dark *by the sense of direction*, by pointing your pistol in the direction in which you conjecture the object to be, not attempting to see your sights or to "draw a bead."

One can often see an animal on a very dark night by crouching down and getting it against the sky-line; and yet, on looking through the sights, you cannot discern anything.

One form of practice is to have a target made of tissue paper, with a candle behind it to illuminate it. The sights are consequently seen in silhouette against it. This was the principle of the "Owl" series of prizes shot for in the early days of Wimbledon in the evenings. What I think better, so as to teach shooting by *sense of direction*, is to have one or more metal targets about a foot square hung by wires (these will give out a ringing sound when struck, and the rest of the butt should be of sand, or sods, or wood, so as to make a different sound). Have a small sleigh-bell hung behind the middle of each target, operated by strings held by an assistant standing behind you.

Now, let him ring the bells at random, you firing by sense of direction towards where you hear each bell ring.

This practice can also be done in a shooting-gallery at night with all the lights turned down, and it is perhaps safer there than out-of-doors.

You can even have targets behind you, and swing round and "snap" at them; but this, and in fact all night shooting, is very dangerous, unless you can be absolutely certain that the bullets will do no damage, however wildly they may fly.

A man with a good ear can do surprisingly accurate work in this style of shooting.

Such practice can be done in daylight by being blindfolded; and then your assistant can notice where your misses go, and help you to improve your shooting.

Footnote

[1] At Bisley a bullet must *cut* the bull to count; at the clubs if it *touches* it scores a bull.

Lightning Source UK Ltd.
Milton Keynes UK
UKHW040613010922
408166UK00004B/342